THE CINNAMON MINE

The Cinnamon Mine

AN ALASKA HIGHWAY CHILDHOOD

Ellen Davignon

Lost Moose in an imprint of Harbour Publishing Ltd.

Harbour Publishing
P.O. Box 219, Madeira Park, BC, VoN 2Ho
www.harbourpublishing.com

All photographs courtesy Ellen Davignon, except where noted.
Cover, top: Johnson's Crossing and Teslin River Bridge; bottom: Betty Porsild with younger sister Ellen and Polly the dog.
Cover design by Anna Comfort
Text design by Cyanotype
Printed on FSC certified paper using soy-based ink
Printed and bound in Canada

BRITISH
COLUMBIA
ARTS COUNCIL

THE CANADA COUNCIL | LE CONSEIL DES ARTS
FOR THE ARTS | DU CANADA
SINCE 1957 | DEPUIS 1957

Harbour Publishing acknowledges financial support from the Government of Canada through the Canada Book Fund and the Canada Council for the Arts, and from the Province of British Columbia through the BC Arts Council and the Book Publishing Tax Credit.

Library and Archives Canada Cataloguing in Publication

Davignon, Ellen, 1937-
The cinnamon mine : an Alaska Highway childhood / Ellen Davignon.

ISBN 978-1-55017-517-2

1. Davignon, Ellen, 1937- —Childhood and youth. 2. Porsild family.
3. Frontier and pioneer life—Yukon. 4. Yukon—Biography.

I. Title.

FC4023.1.D38A3 2011   971.9'103092   C2011-901232-4

To the memory of my mother, Elly Rothe-Hansen Porsild, and my father, Robert Thorbjorn Porsild. "The parents' life is the child's copybook."

ACKNOWLEDGMENTS

LEST THE READER BE MISLED into believing that this composition was dashed off in one single orgy of remembering, the author hastens to inform that *The Cinnamon Mine* did not flow full bore from the nib of her trusty 79 cent Bic. It dripped out, word by premeditated word, as she was pressed and prodded by the following people.

Many, many thanks to Cal Waddington, president of A-V Action Yukon, ex-CBC producer, ex-lodge owner/operator, ex-school chum, who cut short the author's moaning and bleating with a kindly belt in the chops and a terse, "Just go and *do it!*"; the Explorations Program of the Canada Council, which provided her with financial assistance and incentive: "Okay—what do we have to show for it so far?"; Patty Denison and Norm Paulsen—they know why—and the author respectfully requests a speedy descent from their perch on her back; her sisters, Betty Seaborne and Jo Brown, and her brother, Aksel Porsild, who were not a lot of help in the fond memories department but their constant threats to sue did inspire accurate recounting; her children, Toby, Jo, Lise, Jordan and Keeley Davignon, for their interest and loving support, and for keeping their outraged cries of "Whaddya mean I'm not in it?" to a minimum; her husband, Phil Davignon, for his care and attention lavished above and beyond the call.

A painting by Norm Paulson shows Johnson's Crossing Lodge as it appeared in 1992.

TABLE OF CONTENTS

Prologue   11

1. "How dear to my heart..."   13

2. "On the road again..."   23

3. "Be it ever so humble..."   37

4. "I wandered around and finally found..."   47

5. "We didn't find it there..."   61

6. "A place in the summer sun..."   79

7. "Use your imagination..."   93

8. "My mama done tol' me..."   103

9. "Life gets teejus, don't it?"   115

10. "Each mornin' at the mine..."   125

11. "We sang in the sunshine..."   137

12. "...and, my goodness how she'd grown!"   151

13. "Even though we ain't got money..."   163

14. "I'll take you home again..."   175

Epilogue   187

PROLOGUE

I WASHED MYSELF OUT THE kitchen door and hung up the mop on its hook in the porch. "Goin' for a walk," I hollered to my husband and went out into the soft June night. The sun was still high over the western horizon at ten o'clock but there was a coolness to the air that felt good on my face. Washing that big floor always raised a dew on my brow and brought a flush to my cheeks. I started for the highway.

"Hi there, going for your evening constitutional?" Denise Haye came out of her small holiday trailer carrying a light sweater. "Do you mind if I come with you?"

"Not at all," I answered without hesitation. "I'm always glad to have company." She was a nice lady, a widow travelling by herself to Alaska. We had talked a bit earlier when I had registered her and got her settled into the campground, and she had been interested in our old lodge building, the country and the people who lived here. Now, several hours later, we walked together across the bridge and up the gentle hill through the cutbank on the other side of the river.

"You see that?" I pointed at the patch of rusty sand near a gully in the bank. "That was our cinnamon mine." I chuckled at the expression on Denise's face. "Sure. I mined cinnamon out of there till I was fifteen years old."

"And I always thought cinnamon came from the bark of a tree," she said with a little laugh. "Maybe Yukon cinnamon is different." She was quiet for a moment. "Funny about your mine, I suppose you really thought that was what you had. At least until the first taste…"

"Yeah," I agreed, "it was something like my mud pies… looked wonderful, truly good enough to eat. It was strange, though. We *knew* it was only sand but it got to be such an important thing in our lives, our mine, and I really did come over here and dig and make roads until I was well into my teens."

"It must have been lonely for you kids, coming out here away from your friends to this hole in the bush. How did you handle it? For that matter, how did you happen to come out here in the first place? Forty years ago there couldn't have been much here. And after all that time, you're *still* here? How did it all come about?"

I sat down on the low concrete curb at the end of the bridge and thought for a long moment. "Well," I began, "this wasn't the future we had planned, my brother and I. We were going to go into business together one day, and live in a brick house. But it was just going to be the two of us and…"

I

"How dear to my heart..."

IT WAS GOING TO BE AN ENORMOUS house, rusty-red brick with silvery-green ivy clambering up the walls and over the balcony from which we would view our domain as the golden sun sank in the hills and the toil of a long day was over. A huge mountain ash, all glossy leaves and scarlet berry clusters, would guard the front entrance and an ornate wrought-iron fence would delineate the expanse of gently rolling grounds. Stands of blue spruce and masses of daisies would provide welcome islands of colour. And an old oaken bucket, iron-bound and moss-covered, would hang from the rough wooden beam above the fieldstone collar of a deep-water well.

After a while, we would stroll arm in arm down a worn cobblestone path to a small turquoise pond. A weathered old mill might possibly be situated off to one side, its big wheel creaking and sighing and doing whatever it is that millwheels do, gently rippling the still surface as we'd row round and round, laughing softly and making plans for the morrow. On shore, romping joyously and eagerly awaiting our return, would be dozens and dozens of Doberman pinschers. We would be raising them, you see.

Of course, we didn't have an idea in the world what we would be raising them for. Nor had we any idea how or where all this would be taking place. But we did know when. Someday. As my brother Aksel had put it when we had first conceived the idea,

Left to right: Betty, Aksel and Ellen, bundled up like mummies against minus-forty temperatures.

"Someday, Ellen, we'll live together, just you'n me, in this big house. And we'll have lots and lots of Doberman pinschers." (I'm not too sure about the reasoning behind the Dobermans except that Andy Young, the school custodian, had one, a sleek, good-tempered female that Aksel adored.)

"Yeah," I breathed, "and a lake and a boat and stuff."

Aksel stopped dead still in the middle of the path and turned to me, his clear blue eyes slightly out of focus as he concentrated on the future. "And I'll come home," he didn't say from where, "and you can have lunch ready." A fleeting vision of an elegant meal set upon a gleaming dark-wood table rose in my mind. Not jam sandwiches or pea soup, but something all pale green and rose pink set against a backdrop of a towering chocolate layer cake festooned with deep swirls of whipped cream. I swallowed hard.

"Yeah," I said, "and I'd be dressed in a long red dress. And a ruffly white apron."

"No you wouldn't, stupid. If you were helping raise Dobermans you'd be wearing those pants with the bulges on the leg, just like that lady wore in the show last week. And I'd be wearing a big hat, with a brim all round, and smoking those thin cigars."

We resumed our march along the well-travelled trail on the southern outskirts of Whitehorse, each lost in private dreams. "Hey, Ellen," Aksel burst out, "hey, Ellen, and Weldon would come home with me and say he wanted to have seven Dobermans. And say we would sell them to him!" Sell? That would mean money, wouldn't it? Maybe eleven or fourteen dollars! "And we could buy a car. Or even a horse with it!" Holy! This was something we had not even considered. Money. We walked in silence for a moment.

A thought occurred to me. "Aksel, if we sold the Dobermans for money"—another vision, one of gold coins glinting in heaps and piles on the dark table against half a chocolate cake with all the whipped cream eaten off—"if we sold the Dobermans, where would we get more dogs from?"

My brother studied on that for a moment as we trudged along. "Well, we could buy some more somewhere." More studying. "And then, after a while, when we got tired of them we could sell them for more money!" he continued triumphantly. Money would be rolling in. We stood still a bit and beamed at each other. What a splendid idea, the whole thing! The Doberman pinschers. And the big brick house, just like Mrs. Goodings', on Lambert Street, only fancier. And just me 'n Ax, in jodhpurs and boots, living in it, eating pink and green things and chocolate cake, and smoking cigars and counting piles of gold.

But presently the dream had to be shelved because now we were at the top of the hill and there, far below us, was the left lobe of Ear Lake, and lolling on the dirty brown sand, waiting for us on this sunny Saturday morning, were Weldon and Dennis Pinchin. We were only nine and twelve years old, and Someday seemed a far piece down the road. Today, we had to play out the continuing drama of three airmen and an army nurse, shot down in the wilds of darkest Burma.

"Hello, you guys," called the pilot of our downed aircraft, sounding tough and confident, "did you manage to find some grub?" Eagerly I showed him the contents of the paper bag I'd brought. He rummaged a moment and came up with an oatmeal cookie. "Hmm," he grinned, showing sharp teeth, white against the olive of his face, "the natives make cookies just like your mom."

The three of us stood and watched as he devoured the sweet cake, waiting to take our cue from the leader of our little group. "While you were gone," he went on in a hard voice, "the kid and I captured this Jap and tied him to a tree." Weldon gestured and we all turned our heads to glare meanly at the innocent bare trunk of a tall cottonwood. "He'll spill his guts before we're through."

I stared at Weldon with horrified delight. Spill his guts? That was what Robert Walker had said in *Thirty Seconds Over Tokyo*. With some sympathy I looked at the helpless little yellow man. What would we be doing to make him spill his guts, I wondered. Hastily, I sought to change the scene. "Say you were hurt, Weldon, when you caught this Jap and I have to put a bandage on you now."

"Yeah," our pilot's green eyes crinkled in a smile of approval, "good idea, Ellen." I glowed with pleasure and hurried to bind up his wound. "Hey, Ax," he continued, "you men start getting some logs to build a cabin."

Aksel saluted smartly and set off at once, his thin shoulders sharp and straight with purpose. "Come on, Dennis." But Dennis, an intense skinny boy with long arms, and legs that began at his waist, chose that moment to assert himself.

"Go get the logs yourself," he told his pilot. "You always get to be the one doing all the bossing. You never have to... owww..." Dennis' voice rose shrilly as Weldon grabbed his arm and twisted it behind his back.

"You get over there and help Ax. Or go home." He gave his brother a push. Crying more with anger than pain, the younger boy stumbled toward the bush. "You... you... shit!" I gasped at this but Weldon merely turned away, spots of colour high on his cheekbones the only sign of the recent altercation. "Got any more of those cookies?" he asked.

The remainder of the day was filled with battling our way through the dense Burmese jungle, rafting across the narrow breadth of the lake, fending off man-eating crocodiles and poisonous water snakes as we plied our way, and dispatching countless Sons of Nippon in vigorous, valorous hand-to-hand combat.

None of our brave band escaped unhurt and, though I wasn't allowed to fight because only men could do that, I spent most of the time bandaging the grievous wounds sustained during the skirmishes. Weldon, being the biggest and oldest as well as the undisputed leader, bore the worst and most dramatic injuries: a broken arm and not one, but three severed arteries. Aksel, only the co-pilot, was allowed a fractured thumb and facial cuts, and Dennis, in spite of hysterical railings against the fortunes of always having to be tail gunner, was permitted a few superficial lacerations. My moment of glory came toward the end of the day when I tripped over an exposed root and skinned my knee. Dennis hooted at me for being a crybaby, but Weldon wiped my eyes with the tail of his shirt and Aksel let me lean on him while I worked the stiffness out of my genuine injury. I wondered privately if it would be worthwhile falling and skinning the other knee. The little trickle of blood convinced me that it probably wouldn't.

Light was fading fast from the mid-September sky as we fought our wounded way to hell and back. Rumbling stomachs reminded us that we'd best get a wiggle on if we were not to be late for supper.

At a jog, we set out from the jungles surrounding Ear Lake and soon—now a crew of sweaty cowpunchers—we were galloping past the roaring waters of the Whitehorse rapids plunging over the mossy rocks and through spray-dampened undergrowth. With falsetto whoops we trotted out of the woods and onto the railroad tracks skirting the clay banks that followed the curve of the river at the foot of the rapids.

Pete, the ranch foreman, pulled up his magnificent golden Palomino. "Red," he ordered my brother, "cut around to the far side of the herd. Keep the stragglers tight. Kid," he turned as Dennis jolted up on a dusty old pinto pony, "you stay behind in case rustlers are following us." He paused, looked my way, and after a moment spoke respectfully. "You kin ride with me, Miss Sue."

A warm glow swept my face but I just nodded. "Okay, Pete."

Turning to his crew, Pete removed his white stetson from his dark curls, lifted it high above his head and brought it down in a sweeping wave. "Awwwright," he yelled, "let's move 'em out!" Picking up our reins, we started down the tracks at an easy canter, Pete and I in the vanguard, riding easy in the saddle; Red, just slightly back and to the side, keeping his eye on the mavericks as commanded; and the Kid, some distance to the rear, his high-pitched voice alternately urging his little dogies to "git along thar!" and imploring the rest of us to "wait up, you guys!"

Into town we swept, driving the herd of range cows before us onto the broad, relatively empty expanse of Fourth Avenue. Yipping and kiyi-ing, we thundered past the US Army PX, past the Pan American building, past the military hospital and, turning the herd sharply at Lambert Street, rolled between the Anglican church and the school and into the safety of our backyard.

"Good work, men. Nice ridin', Miss Sue," our foreman smiled as we pulled up. Silently we stood for a moment, catching our breath and watching with some pleasure as the scraggly cows milled about, beginning to graze on the lush pigweed that grew rampant along the boardwalk linking our back porch with the outhouse.

"Boy, Ellen, you're gonna get it!" It was my little sister, Johanne, her small, triangular face sharp with malice. "You're supposed to be setting the table tonight and Mummy's doing it." She paused, then looked at Pete and the Kid. "And your mom was here a long time ago, looking for you. She was really mad."

Dennis' normally pale face went white, the freckles over his cheekbones standing out like flakes of copper. A picture rose in my mind of Mrs. Pinchin, a tall dark woman, unsmiling at the best of times, holding my friend by the back of his thin neck with one big hand, the other raised to strike. Dennis and I stared at each other for a single moment, then wordlessly he turned and bolted from the yard, sneakered feet drumming on the board-walk, skinny legs pumping as he rounded the outhouse and flew out of sight down the alley.

Weldon stood a minute longer. "Aw, my mom won't say any-thing," he said confidently. "See you guys later." He sauntered slowly from the yard, pausing at the alley to look back and wave.

"See you, Weldon!" Aksel called. He turned to me. "Holy, Mrs. Pinchin gets madder than Mum. Madder, even, than Dad." The picture came to me again of Dennis dangling from his mother's hand. "Holy," Ax said again, "Weldon isn't afraid of anything!"

"Quick, Ellen." I looked at Jo. "Mummy's waiting for you." I hurried into the house.

"Where have you been?" my mother asked sharply. "It's nearly six o'clock." Speechlessly, I yawped at her standing with her wooden spoon suspended above a pot, her face rosy with the heat of supper cooking on the wood stove. "At Ear Lake again?" She took in my wet shoes and unravelling braids and shook her head, a smile quivering the corners of her thin mouth. "Well, hurry up, wash your hands and finish the table. Aksel," she raised her voice, "bring in an armful of wood when you come."

I went over to the washstand beside the stove and dabbled my hands in the cold water already in the basin, milky blue from a previous washing of hands cleaner than mine. "More!" my mother commanded. Reluctantly, I reached for the bar of strong yellow soap and began to scrub. Boy, I thought to myself, when Ax and I were living in our own house I'd never wash. Or go to bed. Just go swimming in the pond and listen to the radio all night long. Hmm, did radios play all night? I'd have to ask Aksel.

"The table, Ellen!"

Smoothing back my hair with my wet hands, I walked over to see what was needed. Plates. I brought a stack from the pantry and set them around. Glasses. Three trips, two glasses each time, carefully. And the Dipper.

Now, we probably had a pitcher. Or maybe we didn't. I don't remember ever seeing one. But if indeed we had one, we certainly never used it. What held our water on the table was a tin dipper. And not just your ordinary, run-of-the-mill dipper, either, with short handle and pint-sized cup. The Dipper was different— and special.

In the first place, it was big, held water to fill all of our six glasses with enough left over for refills. And in the second place, and far more important, it had a big round handle that jutted from its slanting galvanized side, for the length of ten inches, like a cannon. And like a cannon, we used it against our siblings to spread confusion and terror.

"Mummy," Jo wailed, "Ellen pointed the Dipper at me!"

My mother looked at me with displeasure. "Move it!"

"Well," I began, "she was hoping we'd be in trouble..."

"Move it." My mother's voice was no louder the second time but I reached over and moved the cannon barrel to point harmlessly between Jo and Ax.

Raising my hand to shield my face from my parents' view, I grimaced horribly at my little sister. "Baby," I mouthed silently. Jo turned her face slightly and stuck out her tongue. "Later," I vowed silently. "I'll get you later." Sweet thoughts of vengeance filled my mind as I looked over a tempting array of beef slices on the big cream-coloured platter.

Betty spoke from her place near the far end of the old wooden table. "Hey Ax, where was Weldon going in such a hurry?"

Aksel glanced at me, then turned to face his older sister. "Why?" he asked. "When did you see him?"

"Just before supper," she said. "I saw him up by the cenotaph when I was coming home. He was going like a scared rabbit!"

Later, Aksel and I sat side by side on the boardwalk. He put into words the thought that troubled both our minds. "Do you really think Weldon is afraid of his mom?"

I squinted a bit as a picture of a sharp-toothed, green-eyed rabbit scampering past the war memorial came unbidden, but I shook my head. "Nah," I said. "Nah, Weldon isn't afraid of anything."

We sat companionably. Presently my brother spoke again. "Hey Ellen, did Betty say anything to you about going back to Johnson's Crossing to live? Like we did last summer, only for good. This winter?"

I stared at him in amazement. "To JC? To live?"

"Yeah, she said Mom and Dad were talking about it." Then, "Hey, c'mon, let's ride our bikes for a while."

Later that night I awakened. "...and the mess hall has enough lumber... *mumble*... Johnson's Crossing... *mumble, mumble*..." The drone of my parents' conversation came through the bedroom wall. I strained to hear, lying rigid in my narrow bed and holding my breath till a dry tickle betrayed me and I coughed. The voices stopped. I coughed again and once again. Next door, Dad's feet hit the floor and I heard the soft pad as he came through the dark living room and into the bedroom I shared with Jo. Looming up at the side of the bed, he stood, a hairy giant with a familiar blue bottle in one hand and a spoon in the other.

"Here, sit up and take this," he said softly, pouring out a liberal dose of Buckley's cough syrup. Obediently, I sat up and opened my mouth, hardly even flinching as the virulent white liquid ripped furrows along my tongue and blasted its way to my cough control centre.

"Daddy," I gasped when speech returned, "what were you and Mummy saying about Johnson's Crossing?"

Turning at the door, he looked back at me. "Never mind, now," he said. "Stop coughing and go to sleep." He stumped off.

I coughed again, wetter now that the Buckley's had loosened things up. The undertones resumed in my parents' room. I heard my mother's softer, higher voice. "Has the bank said anything about the loan? What about school...?" I coughed and lost the rest. Dad's voice came again, "...Five hundred... War

Asset Corporation..." *Cough. Cough. Coughcoughcough.* Dad appeared at my bedside again. His hand fumbled in the dimness and presently thrust itself at my mouth. I opened as instinctively as a baby bird and he inserted a dry tablet. "Suck on that!" he ordered and stomped out.

It was an Aspirin, Dad's own personal remedy for most of life's ills and injuries. My tongue, just nicely beginning to smooth out from the Buckley's, shrivelled again, my salivary glands poured juice, and as the acidic moisture hit my throat I coughed again and again, gasping for breath. I heard my mother utter a gentle protest as my father's feet hit the floor with a resounding thud. *Stomp. Stomp.* Our door was opened with some violence and when I looked fearfully in its direction, I could see my father in all his naked splendour, backlit by the pale glow from a streetlight illuminating the window behind him. Patience, not his strong suit at the best of times, was gone and from the doorway he roared at me, "You stop that coughing!"

Buckley's was terrible; Aspirin, worse. But when my father roared, my heart stopped and blood prickled in my veins like ice crystals. As the echo of Dad's booming voice reverberated in our small room, I stuffed the pillow in my mouth, pulled the covers over my head and choked myself to sleep. I would have died before another sound passed my lips. If he could have patented that roar, he might have delivered the world from the common cold. Or at least the cough that accompanies it.

2

"On the road again..."

"OH NO, DADDY!" I CRIED dramatically the next morning upon hearing the confirmation of our impending departure from Whitehorse. "Oh no!" I blubbered, summoning all the heartbreak and pathos my chubby little body could muster. Fat tears welled, just like Margaret O'Brien's in *Meet Me in St. Louis*. "How can I leave my friends? What about school? Brownies?"

Dad ignored me and went on with his plans for the old US Army camp eighty miles south of Whitehorse on the Alaska Highway. My brief moment, centre stage, appeared to have drawn to its natural conclusion so, drooping like a lily, I wandered out and stood indecisively on the back step.

"I'm not going," I thought rebelliously. "They can go all by their own selves, I'm staying here." A brilliant thought occurred. "Maybe I'll run away from home, that'll show them how bad I feel and they won't go." Pensively I peered out through the light drizzle. Somehow, the day didn't seem to be made for running away. So I did the next best thing. I hid behind the massive wooden ironing board in the porch.

Cheered immensely by the thought of all the pain and anguish I would soon be inflicting on my distraught family, I scrunched down comfortably on my haunches and reviewed the situation.

So he had bought it after all. Well, it might not be that bad. There were lots and lots of buildings to explore, windows to break and all that good stuff. Dick and Bud Morris had proven stimulating and imaginative playmates during the past summer months. And Brownies had never really been at issue because I'd been kicked... well... asked to leave, a few weeks earlier after missing four Saturdays in a row to accompany my downed airmen on their valorous adventures.

"I'm really very sorry, my dear, but if you can't be committed to our little group, well then, I'm sadly afraid that our little group simply can't be committed to you." Mrs. Duke had tried for a note of regret but found it difficult to hide the elation that trembled in the downy hairs at the corner of her mouth. "Our little group," to a man, smirked as I was drummed out in a service that was a repeat of one the previous week when I'd been requested to relinquish my membership in the Junior Women's Auxiliary to make room for someone who might be, well, more interested in learning how to do good works.

Mrs. Porter had been hard-pressed to keep from smiling too. But what the heck, my "good works" had always ended up hopelessly tangled and grey with grime, while the only really neat thing the Brownies had been able to impress upon me was their secret incantation of the small brown owl: "To-whit, to-whit, to-whoo. To-whit, to-whit, to-whoo. To-whit, to-whit, to-whoooooo."

To deliver these lines, we had crouched in a circle, fifteen little brown-clad owlets, murmuring softly the words of the first two lines, drawing out the "whoo" on a rising note as we uncoiled slightly. Bouncing back on our haunches, we gathered strength on the second with a more prolonged "ooo" to the "whoo." And on the last line, we leaped vigorously into the air with an ululating "ooooo" that caused Mrs. Duke to fall backwards clutching her ears, and raised the hackles of every wolf within earshot.

"Softly, girls, softly. Like this, ooooo..." This last was delivered in a gently wavering tone.

"A-hooo, a-hooo," I yodelled, then laughed. "Is that right, Miz Duke? A-hooo, a-hooo, arooo..." I stopped, impaled by a piercing glance.

"Thank you, Ellen, for your demonstration of how not to do it. Alright, little owls, let's try again."

Later that evening, I flunked the Good Little Citizen test that Mrs. Duke had prepared for us and, soon after, lost interest in organized hooting. I had liked that ceremony though, and tried to get the boys to incorporate it into one of our scenarios. "Say we were in the jungle and the wolves were all around and we were trying to talk to them…" But only Weldon could make up the plot for the day and my suggestion was ignored.

But now, I'd been behind the ironing board for at least fifteen minutes and boredom was rapidly setting in. Where was Aksel? Why hadn't he come looking for me? I moved restlessly, tired of the view in front of my nose of the rough wooden board with its old sheeting pulled tautly over and secured with safety pins. Idly, I released one, did it up, released it again. My legs were sure getting tired of running away from home in such a folded-up way. Turning sideways, I stretched them out straight and as I did, one heel caught against a small knothole in the floor. I gazed at it with interest. This wasn't just an ordinary knothole; this was the knothole that saved my life every morning when Mom left the kitchen to start whatever it is that mothers do as soon as the kids have been fed and sent off for the day.

Long after Betty and Aksel had gone off to school or wherever, I would still be sitting there, choking and gagging, trying to get down my daily breakfast of oatmeal. Saturdays, we were allowed to have cornflakes. Sundays, when Dad was home he made hotcakes, and when he wasn't, we had tea 'n toast. But every other day of the week Mom made porridge and served it, creamy smooth and glistening with sugar crystals and goodness, to her little family in the knowledge that she was fortifying us against whatever the day might bring. Also, it was cheap. And Betty and Aksel would just slurp it right down in great whacking, cheek-bulging mouthfuls. Jo would pick a little more delicately, nibbling here and there, testing and swallowing daintily until the roses finally showed in her bowl.

"Kin I go now, Mum?" Her small face would lift to her mother, a sweet smile quirking up the corners of her pink mouth. And Mom would gently place a rough hand on her head, gazing down at this wunderkind, her baby, and would smile and nod her head and help her on with her coat and kiss her as she went out the door. Two seconds later she'd poke her head back in, look around for Mom and stick out her tongue at me. "Mum," I'd call, but Jo would be gone, skipping and singing on her merry route to the top of her grade two class in Lambert Street School.

"Oh, Ellen," my mother would groan, looking at the clock, "come *on* now, finish your mush. You're going to be late for school!"

I would look down at my oatmeal, now cold, grey and gluey, and I'd take a tiny bite and force it down with a glass of water and then another wee bit on the end of my spoon. Presently, Mom would finish her coffee and get up from the table to begin her workday.

"You sit right there until you're finished," she'd say, starting upstairs to make up the beds.

I'd wait until I could hear her in Betty's room, then I'd pick up my bowl, tiptoe out to the porch and, with the greatest care and concentration, I'd scrape every last sticky curd down that blessed knothole. Back in the kitchen, I would noisily clatter my spoon against the dish, push back my chair and grab my coat.

"Bye, Mum, I'll see you at lunchtime," I'd call.

"Did you finish your breakfast?"

"Sure, it's all gone." Well, it was. "Bye now."

I peered into the hole now, expecting to see a great slag heap of petrifying mush, but it was dark down there and I couldn't see anything. I sat up again. Where was everybody? Tears started in my eyes. Here I'd run away from home and no one in the world even cared. The tears came in earnest now, making clean gullies down my cheeks and dripping onto my dress. How sad a world when a little girl could run away and be lost and no one would even come searching. Dismally, I crept out of my nest and opened the kitchen door.

The family conference had moved to the kitchen table and Mom was pouring reconstituted Trumilk for all hands.

"Here she is!" she called cheerfully. "Come and have some milk." She pulled out my chair.

As I passed my father he reached out a long arm and pulled me against his side in a warm hug. "What's the matter, Babs? Are you crying about going to Johnson's Crossing?"

Johnson's Crossing? Oh yes, I'd forgotten about that in the subsequent development of my personal crisis. Fresh tears welled. Poor Dad, all he could think of was moving to Johnson's Crossing; he didn't even know how close he'd come to losing his dear little daughter. I saw myself stretched cold and limp on the ground, Dad bending over my body, tears streaming down his sorrowful face. Poor, poor Dad. I turned my face against his shoulder and sobbed.

My father picked me up and sat me on his knee. "Don't cry," he said, mopping my eyes with a big red handkerchief. "It will be fun out there... remember the good times you had with the Morris boys?"

He paused and my thoughts turned momentarily to Dick and Bud. Dad wouldn't have been nearly as pleased, I reflected, about those good times with the Morris boys if he had known what some of those good times had entailed, showing and telling and the like, under the high crawl spaces of the old buildings.

"And," he continued, "we'll have all kinds of people coming in to visit when we open the café. And," he paused again dramatically, and his eyes laughed down into mine, "and with all those long buildings, each of you can have your own bowling alley!" he finished triumphantly. "What do you think of that?"

Stunned, I sagged against him, overcome with the great good fortune that was about to come our way. Our own bowling alley. No, not alley... alleys. Plural. One for each. Oh biff, bang, banjo-eye, Johnson's Crossing, here we come!

A week later, we were loading the truck, locking the doors and preparing to leave for JC, as we had begun thinking of it, "Johnson's Crossing" being a trifle cumbersome in everyday conversation.

It was nearly noon in spite of plans for an early start. Dad was off taking care of some last-minute arrangements and Mom was muttering as she rummaged through the food boxes for cheese and bread, "...don't know why he couldn't have done that long ago... makes me sick... *mutter*..." We kids had now run the gamut of stomach-aching excitement through to boredom at the interminable delays and were now clustered around our older sister, who would not be coming with us.

The little school at the Brook's Brook maintenance camp went only as far as the eighth grade and Betty, a mature sixteen-year-old high-school student, would be staying in Whitehorse, boarding with friends for the remainder of the year.

Bet was a tall, sturdy girl with masses of curly, honey-brown hair and a charming smile that punched a deep dimple at the corner of her mouth. She had inherited her father's temperament—impatient, stubborn and fearless—and the two of them had stood toe to toe on many occasions as she forged the way for the rest of us through Dad's spartan dictates. From reasonable bedtimes to bubblegum, lipstick and dating, she had done the spade work and, as a result, we always had it a trifle easier than she did. But don't think she didn't exact payment. She did. Quite a bit older and a lot bigger, she regarded us as necessary evils and took advantage of our youthful energy every chance she got.

"Ax, get me a glass of water!"

"Ellen, go downstairs and find my math book. And hurry up."

"Jo, tell Mum I'm going over to the Keobkes'."

And she was quick to punctuate a command with a little physical persuasion too. *Slap. Whop. Pow.* "You brats, take that!"

Of course, we asked for most of it, made life miserable for her, every opportunity, just because that's what little brothers and sisters do best, pester and annoy and sass back. "You're not the boss-a me!" we'd yell stridently and run like hell. And we'd steal her gum and candy and comics. On one recent occasion, I'd even stolen her bra.

It was the previous Sunday morning and we'd just waved Mom and Betty safely off for their last time together in the Old Log Church.

"Okay, they're gone, Ellen. Go and get it."

I quickly ran upstairs, rummaged among my sister's under-wear and socks and, moments later, handed Aksel the brassiere.

"Good!" He nodded several times. "Should work really good."

We went out just as Weldon and Dennis Pinchin came by the outhouse and into the yard. Ax handed the bra to Weldon, who stretched it around himself and grinned, looking down at the deflated cups. "Don't fill 'er up too much, do I?" We all laughed, then got down to the serious business.

Pulling down the limber tips of two small poplars growing side by side, the boys secured them to the boardwalk with staples made of bent-over nails. Then they filled the cups of the bra with a miscellany of objects: tacks, nails, apple cores, anything that would wreak death and dismemberment among the rustlers who lay in wait just over the hill, biding their time for an attack on the herd. Now the boys were working with pieces of twine, tying the brassiere straps to the bent saplings. Suddenly, and without warning, another enemy struck from behind.

Betty had returned through the front door, looking for her purse, which had been left on the kitchen table. As she was pick-ing it up, she glanced out the window to check on us, know-ing from previous experience that we were probably up to no good at all. Her idle glance sharpened as it fastened on the object strung between the two trees. Seconds later we looked up to see her bearing down upon us like a juggernaut, all rightful indigna-tion and awful wrath. Springing up with little cries of terror, we attempted to get out of her way but she was everywhere at once, pummelling and smacking and grabbing hair with both hands.

None of us escaped and we all had our share of bruises to examine and compare as she steamed off to take her place in the cool sanctity of the little church, there to assure Mr. Chapple that she was indeed "...in peace and harmony with her fellow man..." as she stuck out her tongue to receive the white communion wafer.

"Boy, I thought she was never gonna stop hitting us." Dennis tenderly felt a blue welt on the back of his thin upper arm. "I was really scared."

"Me too," I murmured. "You too, hey Ax?" He nodded.

"Well, I wasn't scared," Weldon said. "When she hit me, I just stood there. I shoulda hit her right back."

The two younger boys and I stared at him. He'd been cringing and scrambling, just like the rest of us.

Dennis started to tell him so. "Aw, come on, Weldon, you weren't standing there, you were trying to run just like the rest of us... owww!"

Weldon hit his arm again. "I was not, I was just standing there, wasn't I, Ax?" Aksel stared at the ground and didn't answer. "Anyway, let's get this herd over to the ranch, Red. You and the Kid..."

But today, all we could think about was that she was our big sis and we loved her and she was staying behind. Jo had her pipestem arms wrapped around Betty's neck in a stranglehold and tears trembled in her blue eyes. "But you could go to school with us at Brook's. Or Mum could teach you. And we'd never be bad to you again."

"Yeah," Betty laughed derisively, "I'll just bet you wouldn't." She loosened the arms and set Jo down. "Now, don't cry, babe, I'll be home every weekend. Come on, don't cry. Look, here comes Dad!"

We all turned to regard our father as he came striding solidly down the sidewalk, footfalls echoing hollowly on the thick boards.

"All set?" he asked. We nodded. He took the bread and cheese my mother held out to him. "*Tak, min skat,*" he smiled, kissing her cheek. "Thanks, my darling. Ken's going to bring the rest of my tools and the piano when he goes to Teslin tomorrow."

My mother smiled at him, still annoyed but relenting in the face of his obvious good humour. "Don't talk now, just eat. If we wait any longer we have to go tomorrow." She went over to Betty and stood looking at her. One hand reached up and smoothed back the feathery curls from Bet's forehead. On tiptoe, she leaned forward and pressed her lips where the curls had been. "And you be a good girl. Study hard."

Betty's arms went around Mom's ample waist in a hug. "Don't worry, Mom, I will." Her clear eyes passed over us and found Dad. "Bye, Dad. You'll come to see me when you come to town?"

He held her tight against him for a long moment, his eyes moist. "I'll see you," he promised. Releasing her, he fumbled for his handkerchief and blew his nose in a series of little chuffs. "Now, all of you, into your places and let's be off!"

We had been standing entranced by the sad little farewell scene, but now we sprang smartly to do as we were told. Jo giggled with delight. "Look at Jiggs!" she cried, pointing toward the old truck, groaning and creaking with the enormous weight of our worldly possessions. There, on top of the load, stood our big orange tomcat, tail bent rakishly at the tip and tattered ears laid back in mistrust as he investigated his way over the assorted bumps and lumps under the brown tarpaulin. And well he should have looked distrustful.

With Dad's complete faith in his own methods of organization and his callous disregard for the law of gravity, our household goods had been loaded on the truck willy-nilly, smaller items jamming bigger ones to keep everything firmly in place. Mom's old hand-cranked Singer was perched precariously atop the square cabinet of the gramophone, secured only by a slender rope threaded through the handle of the carrying case. Several pots and a large black frying pan were strung along the same line to clang and clatter against the two-by-sixes nailed the length of the flat deck to further support the load. Goods and chattels for a family of six, plus whatever odds and ends Dad had felt might possibly come in handy ("We might never use it but we always got it!") piled layer upon layer on the deck and hung over the sides and end like an over-risen loaf of bread. Only the tarp, a few thin strands of hemp and Dad's frequent commands to "Stay there, you son-of-a-bitch!" held it all in place. Dad walked around the truck, snapping the taut lines and adjusting a few lumps.

"All abooaaard!" he called jovially.

Mom took one more look at the old log building that had been our home for the past several years. "Goodbye, house." She kissed Betty again, pulled my toque down more firmly over my forehead, buttoned the top button of Aksel's coat and allowed herself to be handed ceremoniously into the cab of the old five-ton White.

"There you are, Madame. And here is your baby." Dad swung Jo, light as fireweed fluff in his big hands, onto the seat beside her and slammed the door. "Okay you two, up on the back."

Aksel and I had been watching the alley, waiting for the Pinchin boys. We had spent most of the previous evening with them, involved in the defence of Whitehorse from an all-out attack by German Messerschmitts. The anti-aircraft gun by the cenotaph had belched smoke and flame as we gallantly stood off at least half of Goering's air force and finally drove them from the Yukon's October skies. Afterwards, I had bound up Dave Dawson's broken arm and severe scalp laceration and removed the bullet from Freddy Farmer's torn calf. The radio man, better known as the Kid, had required only a wee daub of iodine for a scratch on the cheek. "Coulda got my eye, hey Dave? Coulda ripped my cheek wide open, hey you guys?" Weldon had ignored him. "Good work, Cherry Ames, army nurse." He smiled at me approvingly, as we abandoned the bomb-blasted turf behind Pinchin's Bakery. "See you guys tomorrow, before you go."

We separated into two groups to fight our way through enemy lines to our respective homes.

Now we were ready to go and they still had not arrived.

"Up with you!" Dad boosted me to a tiny ledge beside the gramophone and held me in precarious place as I scrambled for a handhold. Hooking a leg over an anonymous protuberance, I hauled, Dad pushed, and presently I landed, dress up around my ears, in the snug haven at the front of the load where the faded old sofa had been placed for Aksel and me to ride on. Several bedrolls had been opened out to be tucked around us and I pushed them to one side and slithered over as Ax slid over the top to land, with a thump, beside me. Right behind came Jiggs, the cat, skittering down the hole and into the bowels of the load where he crouched, muttering and complaining, for the entire trip to JC. He didn't like any of this foolishness, not one bit.

Standing on the arms of the sofa, we rose up to peer over the load. Dad smiled up at us. "Okay?" We grinned back, "Okay!" He kissed Betty's cheek. "Bye-bye," he said and gave one last look around, one last poke to the load, and climbed into the cab.

For several seconds the starter ground fitfully as we stood there looking down at Betty. Finally the engine caught with a tremendous roar and moments later, popping and banging, our gypsy wagon began its ascent of the small hill toward Fourth Avenue.

"Goodbye," we yelled, "goodbye, goodbye!" Betty raised her arm in a swooping wave and as we rounded the corner she turned to walk the other way, a curious little skip to her step.

As we approached Main Street on our way out of town, Aksel bumped my arm. "There they are!" he cried, beaming with relief as Weldon and Dennis rode out of the alley on their bicycles and joined us on the first leg of our journey. Laughing, they rode along beside us until they could no longer keep up. A choking cloud of blue smoke blasted from the exhaust as Dad geared up a notch and we watched our friends grow smaller and smaller and with a final wave, disappear from sight. We sank down into our nest.

"Well, they came," Aksel said in a funny voice. I looked at him. "Don't cry, Ax," I said, my own voice wobbly with shared emotion. He rubbed his face. "I'm not crying, stupid. The wind got in my eyes."

We sat in silence, tucking the eiderdowns more snugly around our shoulders.

Aksel spoke again. "Hey, Ellen, say we've got our Dobermans hitched up and I'm driving them and you're riding in the sleigh and we're taking the mail to Dawson."

"Yeah," I added enthusiastically, "and pretend we have to stop and make lunch"—somehow we had missed out on the bread and cheese—"and I cook us some chicken..."

Four hours later we had been to Dawson, delivered the mail in spite of the minus-forty-degree temperature and not one, but three howling blizzards, and were now on the Oregon Trail rolling westward ho! in a lumbering Conestoga wagon. The stage was set for an Indian attack when we felt the truck slowing, coming to a stop. Dad opened his door and stiffly clambered out. "There she is!"

Aksel and I hauled ourselves to the top of the load and looked down into the valley in the direction of his pointing finger.

There she was, indeed. Johnson's Crossing. The long bridge over the wide blue Teslin River. The high clay banks, glowing golden in the slanting October sunshine and on the near side, our side, a broad clearing set with row upon row of long buildings, each a potential bowling alley. We turned to each other and grinned.

Dad slid his arm around Mom's waist as she joined him at the side of the road. "Well, skat, shall we go down and have a look-see?" She rubbed her cheek against his shoulder. "I think we should." She smiled up at us. "Are you ready?"

Looking south from the bridge over the Teslin River, the high clay banks glow golden in the slanting sunshine.

"Ready!" we chorused.

"Then, let's go down," Dad said simply.

He helped Mom back into the cab where Jo slept, unaware of the drama of the moment, then got behind the wheel and released the brake. Moments later, we eased around the gentle curve at the bottom of the hill, bumped over the edge of the road into a large clearing and trundled to a halt in front of a black tarpapered Quonset hut.

We were home.

3

"Be it ever so humble..."

IN THE WARM SUNSHINE WE stood looking around like refugees arriving on a foreign shore. For a time no one spoke or moved. Then a loud, harsh voice broke the spell. "Goddammit, Hazel, bring me the goddam crowbar!"

"What the hell..." Dad muttered and started toward the sound of the voice with a vigorous stride. We followed, a few paces behind, Aksel and I trying to catch up, Mom following more slowly, holding a sleepy Jo by the hand. We rounded the end of a Butler hut.

There, backed against the wooden steps leading into the building, was a dilapidated green pickup, its peeling wooden box brimming with sheets of plywood, two-by-fours and a good assortment of electrical fixtures. Putting his hand on the end of the truck, Dad vaulted lightly to the top step, silently lifted the latch and opened the door. We peered in.

Inside, with his back to us, a short stocky man was balanced precariously on the narrow floor joist, working busily with pry bar and claw hammer levering up a section of plywood flooring. A small mousy woman stood watching nervously.

"What do you think you're doing?" my father asked quietly.

"Yowp!" The man's foot slipped from the joist and plunged through to the ground three feet below. His other foot stayed up, trapped between the floor and the crowbar. "Goddammit,

Hazel," he screamed. "Move the goddam crowbar, quick, afore I get a goddam rupture!"

At the sound of Dad's voice, Hazel had fallen against the wall, her hand clutching at her skinny neck, eyes round with shock. Now she recovered and sprang to help her man.

"Here," Dad said brusquely, "I'll do it." He twisted the iron bar to the side. As he did, the trapped foot came free and the short man groaned with relief as the pressure on his crotch slackened.

"Thanks, Bud," he said ungraciously. "Jeez, you shouldn'ta sneaked up on a guy. Goddammit, I mighta broken somethin'."

Dad smiled grimly. "You already have. You've been trespassing and stealing. That's two broken laws where I come from."

"Whaddya mean, trespassin', stealin'? Nobody owns this stuff."

"Well now, that's where you're wrong. My name is Porsild. I own this camp and I own the material in your truck. And you are trespassing *and* stealing!"

"Aw goddammit, that's news to me," the man blustered. "Everyone's been takin' this stuff." He brushed past Dad and went out to stand on the step, looking at his load and shaking his head.

"Well, from now on you can tell everyone that if they are found on my property, they will have to deal with me." He towered over the shorter man, his pale blue eyes icy with anger. "Now unload your truck and get out!" He stood to one side as the fat man, his face red with rage, climbed into the box and began throwing out lumber and fixtures.

"There," he sneered as he threw down the last sheet of plywood, "you satisfied?" He jumped down and stalked over to the cab, opened the door and squeezed under the wheel. "Goddammit, Hazel, you comin'?"

While the unloading was going on, Mom had risen to the occasion of her first company, welcome or not, introducing herself to the anxious little woman and making small talk in her easy way, ignoring the tension between their two men. Now, at the sound of the rude summons, they both jumped. Hazel scuttled over to the truck, which was already starting to move, and opened the door.

She managed to get in, and as the vehicle picked up speed she rolled down the window. "It was nice meeting you..." she called back through the dust. Mom raised her hand in an airy wave.

"Goddammit, Hazel was a nice little lady, hey Mum?" Mom looked down at Jo. "Yes," she cleared her throat. "Yes, honey, she was." She turned to Dad, who was mumbling under his breath and sliding plywood into a pile. "Maybe we should look at the rest of the buildings," she suggested.

Dad straightened from his task, nodded and led us on our investigation. He opened the flimsy slatted door on the next building for our inspection. It was dim inside the musty hut, the light from the windows diffused by the opaque painted wire screening that filled them, in place of glass. My heart sank. Some bowling alley! It was long enough, of course, but all that remained of the lanes were the cross-braces that had once supported the plywood floor. Above the bare bones, vandalized light fixtures swung gently to and fro in the draft.

"Goddam bastards!" Dad growled.

We went on, taking stock. Each of the Butler huts had been damaged or stripped to some degree. Sections of flooring had been removed from most, as had doors and windows. The five Quonsets had fared better, being closer to the highway, and the enormous mess hall, T-shaped and of frame construction, had survived mainly intact.

"This would make a good bowling alley," I said, standing in the middle of the long dining hall. Dad looked at me questioningly. "Remember? You said we could each have our own bowling alley? You said..."

Dad's face cleared and he laughed. "Yes, I guess I did, didn't I? But first, we'd better find a place to sleep before we go bowling." We trooped out of the chilly building and quick-stepped back to the Quonset huts. Mom glanced into all five.

"This one is the cleanest," she said decisively, indicating one in the second row. "We'll use it as a bedroom. And that one," pointing to the one closest to the road, "will be the café." She looked inquiringly at Dad.

"You heard the boss," he chuckled, beginning to loosen ropes on the load. "Ax, get up here and start handing down…"

Setting up a home was child's play for my mother. Over the twenty years that she and Dad had spent together, she had made a home in a reindeer camp in the Arctic, in a small cramped house on the Vancouver waterfront, in an assortment of log cabins along various Yukon rivers and, for at least one summer, in a tent on a raft on the Stewart River. Turning a well-insulated, elongated igloo-shaped Quonset hut into a cosy place wherein to hang our hats would be no problem at all.

"First of all, Aksel, find my broom." Ax burrowed into the load. "Bob, take these boards out of here and tie up those fixtures. Ellen, you and Jo take this pail down to the river and get some water. And be quick, we don't have all day."

And indeed we hadn't, what with it being mid-afternoon and night coming down quickly this time of year. By the time Jo and I had struggled back from the river, losing half our water but richer for the detailed examination of a porcupine we had encountered on the way, the hut had been transformed into a snug chamber.

The low rounded interior had been divided into two areas by hanging a pair of faded burgundy drapes on a wire from one wall partway to another. One side of this partition was to be my parents' room. Their big double bed had been made up with Dad's heavy Woods sleeping bag across it and a familiar faded pink chenille spread over that. Bright rag rugs made spots of colour on the rough flooring, and on Dad's side a wooden packing crate stood on end to serve as a night table. Mom's golden oak dresser, with its wavy-glassed mirror set in an ornately scrolled frame, sat with its back to the end wall, too high to fit against the curving side of the building. Dad's old green-painted highboy stood tall by the drapes, reinforcing the privacy of their little corner of the world.

Half a dozen starched housedresses hung on hangers from a nail beside the dresser. A ceramic frog ashtray, a spent cigar butt smouldering on its tongue, squatted on the packing box and, over it, pinned top and bottom to conform with the concave wall, was Billie.

Billie was a testimonial to my mother's love and forbearance. A lusty nude calendar girl, the glossy print—Dad's "girlfriend"—had accompanied him all over the North, gracing log cabins and tent walls alike with her soulful gaze and golden skin. From Sixtymile to Dawson to Snag and Norman Wells, she had travelled with him, and now, a bit worn and showing the ravages of time, she had come to his new home on the banks of the Teslin River.

We never knew where Billie had come from, and when we asked Mom why she let Dad have a naked lady she merely smiled and said something about her being Dad's girlfriend, and we let it go at that. It was not until we were a lot older that Betty pointed out the similarities between Billie and Mom. "Look at this picture of Ma. See the way her hair curls over her cheek. And her eyes are nearly the same. And the mouth." Of course, it was harder to equate Billie's lean curves with Mom's short, round figure, but on a dark trail, far from home, I have a feeling that the two melded perfectly in Dad's mind.

The other half of the building had been set up for the three of us. Jo's wooden bed, with its white high-slatted sides, and two army cots had been put side by side under the curve of the wall. Each had its own covering of eiderdown and chenille. Braided rugs filled the spaces between the beds and against the opposite wall another cot had been placed, its thin mattress covered with a cotton throw. Several cushions were heaped to make a comfortable place to read and daydream, and on weekends it would be Betty's bed.

An airtight heater, its pipes not yet installed through the slanting roof, sat near the extra bed and beside the frog on the crate and on a large dresser at our end of the hut stood tall kerosene lamps, their glass chimneys sparkling with recent polishing, their heavy bases glowing amber with the oil that would light our way to bed.

Outside, Dad had arranged the tarp from the truck over a frame, and under it, Mom's little kitchen range belched smoke from its truncated chimney as she reheated the stew she had prepared the day before. On the back of the stove, the half-filled galvanized pail steamed. The chipped enamel wash basin had been set on an upended log, yellow soap close by on another stump, and on a bare willow branch, conveniently close, hung a threadbare towel.

The lid of the big food box was closed and over it Mom had draped a cotton tea towel, the words "Robin Hood" still showing faintly pink against its bleached whiteness. On this impromptu buffet was a stack of china plates, creamy white with rosebuds and bluebells around the rim, an assortment of mismatched knives and forks and, its cannon barrel pointing innocently at no one in particular, the Dipper, filled to the brim with cold river water. A scored pine breadboard supported a crusty loaf of whole wheat bread cut into several thick slices and, beside it, a tin container, its hinged lid thrown back to reveal its treasure of golden butter. An assortment of beet and cucumber pickles added colour to the scene and a large jar of strawberry preserves completed the picture.

Dad's stomach rumbled loudly as we stood surveying this repast. We laughed uproariously as he patted the offending portion of his anatomy. He looked down at it. "Shhh," he said, "don't hurry the cook, it isn't polite."

The cook glanced up from her labours, cheeks pink and dark hair curling against her forehead. "It's nearly ready."

Dad stepped to her side, slid an arm around her shoulders and, leaning down, kissed her softly on the mouth. We giggled as they stood smiling at each other.

"I allus thought that Billie was your girlfriend, Dad," Aksel chortled.

"She is." Dad kissed Mom again and then released her. "Alright, get washed for supper," he commanded his young brood.

With a minimum of pushing and shoving, we did as we were told, hunger adding speed to our careless ablutions. Soon, we were settled on a variety of logs and benches, watching avidly as Mom began filling our plates with the savoury meat and vegetables.

We had progressed to dessert, thick slabs of bread spread generously with the glistening strawberry jam, when the quiet was broken by shouting and laughter.

"Hi!" shrill boyish voices called. "Hi, you guys!" And around the corner and off the highway, crouched over their handlebars and pedalling furiously, came Dick and Bud Morris.

We jumped up and started over to greet our friends, stopped and came back. "*Tak for mad*, Mum," we chorused politely, as we had been taught to say after a meal. "Thanks for the food."

"*Velbekommen*," she replied, "you're welcome."

Released, we ran out to greet the boys, all of us laughing and talking at once. "How did you know..." "When did you..." "Are you... will you...?" We stopped and stood there, grinning like fools.

Dad sauntered over. "Hello, boys," he said, smiling at them. "How did you know we were here?"

"Well," began Dick, "Dad said he thought he heard hammering, and besides, me and Bud have been watching for you and when I saw smoke I knew you'd come," he finished in a rush, his dark eyes sparkling.

"It was me saw the smoke!" Buddy pushed his brother. "It was me saw it."

"Aw, it was not, it was me."

Dad interrupted. "Well, whoever it was, it's nice to see you again." He stopped as Jack Morris' narrow brown vehicle came hurtling up to our entrance, and lifted an arm in greeting as it turned in and drew up to our little group. "Hello there, Jack." They shook hands through the open window. "Good to see you."

"Hello Bob, I thought maybe you could use some water. I hauled today and had some left over." He indicated the small tanker trailing behind the old US Army carryall.

"It was good of you to think of us." Dad raised his voice, "Elly, bring that pail and the kettle, Jack's brought us some water."

Mom had been tidying up from supper and now she emptied the pail into a dishpan, picked up the kettle and came over to stand by the van.

"Jack, how are you?" she smiled, giving Dad the pails.

"Welcome to Johnson's Crossing. Again." He turned away briefly, then handed her a pan. "The Missus was baking today, thought maybe a crumb cake would go down kinda good." His brown mustache bristled with shy goodwill and he scratched at a mole on the side of his face with a thumbnail. "She said to tell you, you need anything, you've only to ask."

Dad came up to stand beside Mom, pail and kettle sloshing full. "Many thanks, Jack, this will do us, and tomorrow Ax and I will fix up a barrel and get some from the river."

"Okay, Bob, but if you need more..." He hesitated, jerked his head toward the buildings. "Much stuff missing from the camp?"

Dad nodded. "Some," he admitted.

"I came over a few times, ran off some of them thievin' bastards. Guess they came back again."

They stood in silence for a minute.

"Well, best I should be getting back." Jack backed up, jack-knifing the tanker, grinned sheepishly and pulled ahead to circle around, then stopped. "By the way," he called, "if you want, I can take the kids to school on Monday. We're going anyway."

"Thanks, Jack," Dad returned, "but we'll have to go and meet the schoolmarm and get them registered. Maybe we can work something out though, you take them one day and I the next, something like that."

"Right." Jack raised his voice. "Awright, guys, let's go." He pulled out onto the road, blatted the horn once and careened off, dust and gravel flying as he accelerated and was gone.

Dick and Bud mounted their bikes. "Guess we have to go too," Dick said, eyeing the darkening sky.

"C'mon, Ellen," Aksel said to me, "let's go with 'em out to the bridge." We started down the road, the boys riding slowly, Ax and I walking beside them. I looked back at Jo, standing forlornly in the middle of the yard, doll dangling by one leg, dress ties wrapped twice and knotted around her slight body.

"Come on, Jo," I hollered, "you can come too." Belatedly, I looked at Aksel. He nodded. "Come on!" I called again. She started running toward us, knobby knees lifting high and long brown stockings sagging lower with each stride.

"Go on, you guys. I'll wait for her." Bud stared at us defiantly.

"Waiting for your girlfriend, hey?" Dick laughed.

Bud stepped away from his bike, selected a stone and winged it past his brother's ear. "She ain't my girlfriend!" he yelled.

We all laughed and walked on, followed presently by Bud and Jo, walking together as he pushed his bike. At the end of the bridge we stopped and the boys rode on alone, waving and calling goodbyes. We watched until they hit the far end.

"See you tomorrow." The words came faintly. They waved once more and started through the cutbank and out of sight.

We stood a moment longer, leaning on the guardrail watching the river rolling slick as oil through its dark bed far below us. Night was falling down quickly now and, tearing ourselves from the mesmerizing scene, we turned and started back toward the camp. It looked peaceful in the fading light and as we watched, a bald eagle floated over the hill on silent wings, sideslipping against the dark pines, hunting one last small snack before turning in.

"Let's go, you guys!" Aksel whooped. Picking up our reins, we broke into an easy canter and headed back to the ranch. As we galloped into the yard, a big yellow cougar sprang at us from the bushes.

"Hello, polecat!" Ax cried, grabbing it up into his arms. "Where have you been all day?" Jiggs gazed at him with regal disdain, declining such a roughneck invitation to enumerate his adventures. We trooped over to the lean-to where our parents sat talking, cigar smoke pungent in the air as Dad smoked his last White Owl of the day.

"Got anythin' fer a pore hungry bum?" Aksel set the big tom down gently.

"I saved him some stew in that dish." Mom pointed at the food box and watched as Ax put it down for Jiggs. "And now," she said, "I think it's about bedtime."

For once there was no protest. We were eager to test our new sleeping quarters and allowed ourselves to be herded inside without a murmur. Aksel and I began to undress but Jo stood scowling at her small wooden bed.

"Mum, how come I got to still sleep in a baby bed?"

Mom scooped her up and hugged her. "Because," she replied, kissing her on the neck, "because you are still my baby." She began undressing Jo and soon we kids were all in bed, sleepy and snug under the heavy covers. The lamp on the dresser threw soft shadows over us as Mom puttered about, hearing our prayers and tucking us in against the chill night air. Dad stood watching as she kissed each of us. *"Godt nat. Sove godt."*

"Good night. Sleep well."

Dad put his hand behind the lamp chimney, deflecting his breath downward, extinguishing the flame. In the sudden dark Jo spoke again, her soft voice trembling a bit. "Mummy, where is Betty right now?"

"Betty's staying with the McPhails, honey. She has her own room there and everything."

"Oh, that's right, I forgot." Jo was quiet for a moment. "Will she come and see us?"

"Oh sure, she'll be here next weekend." Mom spoke reassuringly. "Be a good girl now and go to sleep."

"'Kay." She rolled over, her leg thumping softly against the sideboard. "Mum?"

"What now?"

"I'm really not a baby anymore. When can I have a bed like Ellen and Ax?"

Mom's voice came drowsily but with a smile in it. "You can have one when you're big. For your birthday. Now go to sleep."

We heard Dad puff out their lamp, a few rustling sounds as our parents settled into their favoured sleeping positions, and soon, the first gentle gargles as Dad began his familiar evensong. We smiled in the darkness.

"Ellen," Aksel hissed.

"What?"

"I'm glad we've come back."

"Me too. G'night."

"'Night."

4

"I wandered around and finally found..."

IT MAY HAVE TAKEN MY FATHER a bit of coaxing and soft-soaping to convince his children that returning to Johnson's Crossing was "meet and right so to do." He had no such problem with his wife. As far as she was concerned, it was not only meet and right, but her bounden duty, whither thou goest and all that. It just took Dad saying, "Come, skat, let's do this for a while," and Mom replying, "Well, why not? We've tried nearly everything else!"

My father was a persuasive charmer, full of energy and wholehearted zeal, with eyes as blue and clear as a winter sky.

My father, Robert Thorbjorn Porsild, known in his early years as Stor Thor (Big Thor) to close friends and family, was a tall, robust man, a persuasive charmer with thick auburn hair and eyes as blue and clear as a winter sky. He was born in Copenhagen but raised in Greenland. His father, Dr. Morton P. Porsild, a Danish scientist of some distinction, had been funded by the Carlsberg Foundation (the beer people) to establish a botanical research station on Disko Island off the western coast of Greenland, and in 1906 he moved his young family to the bleak rock that would be their home for the next thirty years. Thor, his brother Erling and sister Asta, and eventually a much younger brother, Sten, spent their early years roaming as free and unfettered as their Greenlander companions, learning about botany and biology at their father's knee, and about life and love away from it.

Morton P. was something of a martinet, who demanded and received strict obedience and total compliance. He was a stern, chilly man, somewhat cruel and unorthodox in his discipline.

One day, Thor and Erling had been fooling about, as boys will, especially if there is a small gaggle of young girls looking on with admiring eyes. Thor swung a well-honed axe carelessly, Erling held a driftwood log foolishly, and when the smoke and dust cleared, Thor remained standing by the chopping block with anguished eyes while his ashen-faced brother was led off to the house, his hand wrapped in a bloody cloth.

Later, Thor was summoned to his father's study, greeted there by an icy stare as Morton P. stood before him for several silent moments, his hands behind his back. Finally, he spoke.

"Do you know what you have done?"

Thor looked at him, speechless. He licked dry lips but no words came. His father brought one hand from behind his back. "Here," he said, and when his son automatically stretched forth his hand, he put Erling's severed forefinger into it.

But as well as learning about botany, biology and the proper method of splitting kindling, from their Eskimo friends they acquired a proficient knowledge of the native language and spent much of their free time with the Greenlanders, both socially and on their hunts. They mastered the art of controlling the large teams of half-wild huskies that towed the huge sleds pell-mell over the rough sea ice in pursuit of seal and polar bear. They learned to build snow shelters in record time in defiance of Boreas, who would come raging from his northern regions, intent on destroying the mortals who dared to test the limits of his fury. They learned to build kayaks of bone and skin; to construct the marvellously light sleds of caribou hide with frozen whitefish rolled into the edges and turned under for runners; and to gather seabird eggs from the rocky headlands of the Greenland coast.

During this time of growing and learning, there was instilled in them a love and respect of the North and all its people, which would last the whole of their lives.

Those happy and bucolic years, however, came to an end. The need for formal education became evident—one does not, after all, live on seal oil and lichen alone—and Thor and Erling were sent to a boarding school in Denmark. They remained there, apart from their family, for several years and it was during this time that Erling, always a frail boy despite his vigorous upbringing, contracted tuberculosis. The school doctor advised his seclusion in a state-run sanatorium, but in fact he was whistled home by an indignant mother who firmly believed that the good, crisp Greenland air, augmented by liberal doses of maternal solicitude, would be in his better interest. And so they were. Erling made a full recovery from the wasting disease and grew to sturdy and active manhood. He never returned to school in Denmark but continued his scientific studies with his father, eventually becoming Morton P.'s assistant at the Disko Research Station.

Thor, in the meantime, remained in Denmark. Prevented from returning to his Greenland home by the crushing expense of the long sea voyage, he spent many of his weekends and school holidays visiting with friends and relatives. He was a welcome guest, attractive and sunny, with a gift for storytelling that was evident even then. Ultimately, he enrolled in the University of

Copenhagen, where he majored in biology and simultaneously cut a burning swath through the fluttering female population. The combined activities proved too much and he, too, fell ill.

His fainting spells were diagnosed as a mild form of epilepsy. It was suggested that he take time off from his studies to seek some energetic outdoor activities. With the blessing of his concerned, though disappointed, father, Thor left Denmark and sailed for America, California-bound, to visit a cousin who had emigrated there some years before. He was making slow but steady progress in that direction and had travelled as far as Chicago, when he received some bad news. The cousin, he learned, had succumbed to some undisclosed malady, going on to his reward without so much as a passing thought to his transmigrant relative. Becalmed, Thor sat, chin in hand, mulling over such inconsiderate behaviour and listing his potentials.

He still had this troubling ailment that came on him inconveniently, though less frequently. He had very little money and few marketable skills, there being only a scant demand in the Chicago of 1924 for a seal hunter of great bravery or a builder of kayaks, no matter how many grasses he could identify right off the top of his head. What he did have, however, was a strong back and a willingness to work, and soon after this short period of introspection he found gainful employment with the Borden Milk Company.

This job ended in disaster. One afternoon, a seizure sneaked up on his blind side just as he was lifting a case of bottled milk onto a gurney. Borden's wiped the milk from his face, informed him that he was a menace to their tidy and well-ordered operation and regretfully terminated his employment.

Never one to linger over past misfortunes, he soon was back job-hunting and before long was working again. This time he heeded the advice of his physician and for the next two years worked for a country club as a general handyman, grooming the links and maintaining the buildings. For this enjoyable pottering he received a fair wage and in a short time had saved the down payment on a Harley-Davidson motorcycle and a rather dashing leather jacket.

He adopted the name Robert—it seemed to go with the motorbike —and was soon Bob to his new friends. He liked Chicago. He liked the easy-going American people and they liked him.

But now providence took a hand in the fate of Morton P. Porsild's more or less stalwart sons.

The Canadian government had decided to investigate the feasibility of importing reindeer from Alaska to the eastern side of the Mackenzie Delta to start a herding industry and to ensure an adequate supply of meat and skins for the Inuit of the eastern Arctic. The first step was to determine the extent of suitable forage along the proposed migration route and in the areas where the new herds might be located. In 1926, Erling, already well known as an expert in the field of Arctic flora, was hired by O.S. Finney, director of the Northwest Territories and Yukon branch, Department of the Interior, to find a route with sufficient food for the animals during the journey. He eyed the map, licked his chops in anticipation of the virgin study area and made one small request: that his big brother be taken on as his assistant. Finney agreed and two days later Bob received a telegram saying, in effect, "Come a-runnin'." More likely—my Dad's family never having been noted for their brevity—the telegram read something like, "*Komme sa ve skal nu vente tilbage nordvestlig til vaere stor morscab stoppe kaerlighed hilsen lillebro.*" Or, roughly translated, "We're going north for some high old times, stop. Bring snowshoes and Mother's recipe for barbecued muktuk, stop. Love and kisses, your little brother."

Chicago and all his delightful new friends notwithstanding, it didn't take Bob long to make up his mind. The return wire read, "Lead on, McPorsild!" and for the next two years they carried out their investigations, travelling some fifteen thousand miles by foot, canoe and dog team. They returned to Ottawa with approximately fourteen thousand herbarium specimens of vascular plants, nearly five thousand samples of mosses and lichens and about a thousand photographs. On the strength of their reports, three thousand reindeer were purchased from private owners in Alaska.

In 1929, Erling went to Nome to represent the Canadian government in the selection of the herd and the beginning of the drive while Bob went to the Mackenzie Delta to begin making arrangements for the eventual reception of the animals. The rest is a bit of well-known Canadian history.

The drive, which got under way in December 1929, was placed in the capable hands of Andrew Bahr, a veteran Lapp herder. He was assisted by other Lapps and several Eskimos. The route was long, over fifteen hundred miles of difficult terrain, and their progress was impeded by blizzards and severe cold, attacks by wolves and the distraction of wild caribou. But the drive went on, its losses being somewhat recouped with each calving season.

The herd reached the Canadian border four years later but unsuccessful attempts to cross on the glare ice of the Mackenzie Delta delayed delivery until March 1935. Over twenty-three hundred deer were delivered, only a fifth of them remaining from the original stock.

A reserve of sixty-six hundred square miles was created east of the delta. Through the first summer the deer grazed in the coastal area near a corral at Kittigazuit. They were moved inland for the winter and to Richards Island in the spring. By 1936, the herd had exceeded its original number. In the next few years new herds were developed and, finally, the government sold them all to Natives.

In the fall of 1929, Bob went back to Denmark for a holiday. While visiting the small university town of Soro, he met the parents of an old school chum, Svend Rothe-Hansen. They had been entertained by his company many times in the past and they greeted him now with open arms. Quite frankly, I believe Fru Rothe-Hansen took one look at this good-looking red-haired young fellow, gave immediate thought to her eldest daughter withering on the vine in a steamship office in Copenhagen, and began humming the wedding march under her breath. Bob was taken home, primed with roast pork, akvavit and family gossip, and dispatched to Copenhagen with Elly's address embroidered on his shirt front.

You have to know that my grandmother's instincts were good. Before the month was out, Bob was back at the Mackenzie Delta building corrals, overseeing preparations for the delivery of the herd and arsey-turvey in love.

⋅⋅⋅∞⋅⋅⋅

While all this to-ing and fro-ing was being accomplished by the man known variously as Thor, Robert, Bob and, finally, Krungilak (Reindeer Man) by his Eskimo herders, Elly Rothe-Hansen was not exactly sitting on her hands waiting for him. She was the second oldest of nine children born to Julie and Adolphe Rothe-Hansen, a farmer turned manufacturer who had made a fortune during the First World War building fish-packing crates, and lost it soon after through a combination of high living and bad investments. Elly spent most of her young life shepherding her younger brothers and sisters. Later, as did most young middle-class girls of

A high-spirited young woman possessed of a biting wit, Elly was her father's pride and joy but her mother's despair.

her time, she went to live with a variety of families, working for her room and board as a companion or nanny, and learning the whys, wherefores and how-tos of running a household.

The Rothe-Hansen home was a favourite gathering place for young people and, with several brothers bringing home friends, Elly and her sister Gudrun could be fairly choosy about their suitors. Both girls were pretty, high-spirited young women, popular and sought after, but independent and just a tad callous in their treatment of their eager admirers. Elly, in particular, possessed a biting wit and her pale blue eyes smiled easily but could grow cold as snow shadows upon provocation. She was her father's pride and joy but her mother's despair.

"Don't be so cruel to poor Jorgen. He's a nice boy."

"He's an idiot!"

"But you are nearly twenty-five years old."

"Does that make him less of an idiot?"

Elly went from being housekeeper and governess to nursing in a tuberculosis sanatorium. This was interesting and rewarding work but after two years of soothing fevered brows and emptying bedpans, it was time for a change. In rapid order, she took a course in stenography, hired on as a receptionist in a steamship office, shed a fiancé who had failed to measure up, and freshened her mother's desperation. She was nearly twenty-seven years old.

The tall man who knocked at the door of her modest apartment seemed vaguely familiar.

"Yes," she asked sharply, "what is it?"

"Elly?" He looked down at her with laughing eyes. "Elly, it's Thor... Svend's friend." He paused. "Your mother asked me to visit you."

Good old Mother, Elly thought wryly. Aloud, she said politely, "How nice to see you again, Thor." She opened the door wider. "Won't you come in, I was just making lunch."

Thor, or Bob as he insisted she call him, stayed for lunch, afternoon tea, supper and a late evening snack. He returned early the next morning to walk his friend's sister to work and arrived

promptly to retrieve her when the office closed. He wined, dined
and regaled her with tales of high adventure; some, exaggerations
and a few, outright lies. And he looked at that smooth tan face
with its high cheekbones and thin mobile mouth and knew that
this was the woman with whom he wanted to share his hard tack
and dried fish, till the end of his days.

For her part, Elly was equally enchanted, as much by the
romance and drama of his life in another world as by his charm
and good looks. Three weeks after his arrival on her front stoop,
Bob took her right hand and slipped a plain gold band on its
fourth finger. "Will you marry me, Elly, and come to Canada?"

Elly looked at the ring for a moment, then at Bob. She smiled.
"Do you have to ask?"

A week later, Bob returned to Canada to resume his respon-
sibilities at the reindeer station. Elly remained in Copenhagen to
relay the news to her ecstatic mother and prepare for the coming
nuptials, scheduled tentatively for spring.

It was not to be. The Canadian government was not, after all,
a marriage brokerage and since there was this little matter of a
pesky herd of deer due to arrive in the near future, they thought
that perhaps if Bob was hell bent on acquiring a bride, well then,
said bride should come from Denmark to join him in Aklavik
rather than the other way around. And so she did. She packed
her linens and china and a couple of enormous *spiepulse* (a hard,
spicy sausage), chose several sensible dark dresses and a suit of
woollen underwear, added a fetching nightgown or two, kissed
her family goodbye and set sail.

In the meantime, brother Erling had been busy. In addition to
orchestrating the reindeer drive, he was raising a daughter, Karin,
whose Greenlander mother had died shortly after her birth,
and was establishing a permanent base in Ottawa, to which he
brought a new Danish bride, Asta. It was to Erling's Rockcliffe
Park home that Elly now came, staying with Asta and improving
her English while Bob built a house for them on a high cutbank
on the Mackenzie River delta.

It was a time of great excitement and anticipation mixed with boredom and a bit of discontent.

Asta was the daughter of an admiral in the Royal Danish Navy. Elly was the daughter of a farmer, a failed industrialist, now the assistant editor of a small newspaper. Asta prepared sumptuous dinners with a lot of clarified butter and a soupçon of chopped black truffles. When it was Elly's turn in the kitchen, she produced curried beef tongue with rice.

"How very... interesting," Asta commented. "When we served curry in our home, we used Madeira. And olives. This is very... interesting."

But though the young women found little in common, Asta proved to be a good tutor. English was taught in Danish schools in those days but it was most elementary: "I can hop on one leg, can you? Let me see if you can. Yes, that is very good." At the age of twenty-seven and soon to be married, it seemed a tad undignified to be going about challenging new acquaintances to go leaping and bounding, so Elly settled for several hours of linguistics every afternoon and by the end of her stay in Ottawa, her command of English had become better than adequate, if not exactly glib.

Finally, the long-awaited telegram arrived, advising of the completion of the house, the condition of the weather, the preparedness of the church and its minister and the eagerness of the bridegroom, not necessarily in that order. Two days later, Elly was on her way again.

Leaving Ottawa by train on August 15, she arrived in Edmonton three days later. The next day, she climbed aboard the old "Muskeg Special," a somewhat decrepit little freight train that linked the supply city of Edmonton with the headwaters of the Mackenzie and the hardy people who lived along its course, and journeyed north to Waterways. Here, she embarked on the riverboat *Northland Echoes* and travelled down the Athabasca River, across a southwest arm of Athabasca Lake onto the Slave River, and eventually, via a portage of nine miles, into a corner of Great Slave Lake. She boarded the river steamer *Distributor*, exchanged it two days later for the good ship *Mackenzie* and arrived, in due course, to freezing temperatures and a warm welcome in Aklavik.

The whole town had turned out for the arrival of Bob's bride. White women were in short supply all over the North but besides that, Bob was very popular in the small community and all were eager for a glimpse of the woman who was about to hogtie the friendly giant. They were not disappointed.

The trip had been long and arduous but Elly had had the time of her life. Her gaiety and wit had infected all who had travelled with her and her interest in the country, its customs and people, had so charmed the rough and lonely rivermen who travelled the broad Mackenzie that they had gone out of their way to provide her with company and small comforts. She was the picture of radiant health, her cheeks pink with cold and excitement, and her soft chestnut curls blowing about her face as her eyes fastened on the tall form bounding up the gangplank.

Bob swept her up in a massive hug and as he released her to step back for another look, she grabbed his ears and pulled his mouth down to hers. A great cheer went up from the crowd. Krungilak had indeed got himself a woman!

They spent the next three years in the reindeer station on the delta. Bob was absent much of the time, travelling between the herd and the station with supplies, or on dispatch to Ottawa for report of progress or lack thereof. But Elly found friendship and comfort among the families of the Lapp herders and was content. Besides, she had another adventure to look forward to.

Given their brief, almost chance, courtship and the long interval between betrothal and nuptial knot, there should have been at least a short period of adjustment and reacquaintance, getting to know you, tra-la, and all that. It was quite the contrary. Except for a brief discussion of the pros and cons of eating pancakes for breakfast, Bob and Elly came together in the true spirit of compromise and willingness.

My father found work on a Canadian government project investigating the feasibility of importing reindeer from Alaska to the eastern side of the Mackenzie Delta.

My mother joined her new husband at the reindeer station late in the summer and baby Betty arrived the following spring, the first white child born in Aklavik.

Bob's approach to marriage was completely in keeping with his character: wholehearted zeal and joyous application. Within a month of her arrival, Elly was pregnant. At this time, we can only speculate on the excitement this news generated in the Rothe-Hansen household back in the old country. But in the small house on the riverbank, I am sure the information was received far more matter-of-factly.

"Bubi, I think I'm pregnant."

"Well, skat, of course you are. After all that, I would be very surprised if you were not. Come, let's go and make sure."

Elly, though a strong-minded, independent young woman, had led a rather sheltered life and she came to her marriage with an eagerness and thirst that would have daunted a lesser man. Everything had to be tried and tasted: "Don't sit there grinning at me, let's tour the corrals. Come, I want to help you saw driftwood and learn to use the water yoke and after that you can teach me how to drive the dogs." Rather than a hobble on all this season-ing, her pregnancy was welcomed as one more experience to be savoured and enjoyed, concrete evidence of her new life.

Anna Elisabeth arrived the following June, the first white child born in Aklavik.

It was an easy delivery and Betty was a perfect first child. As beautiful as her mother and charmingly imperious as her father, she bloomed like a small pink rose among her sturdy little brown companions at the station. Pleased with the result of this collabo-ration, Elly was soon pregnant again and delivered her second child when Betty turned two.

During this seventh year with the reindeer project, Bob had become increasingly restless. Erling was still very much involved with the drive but had moved his headquarters to Ottawa and the brothers rarely saw each other. With Erling's absence from the field, Bob felt that much of the excitement and adventure had dulled and for the most part his work was done. The corrals were ready; the Natives trained to care for the animals; and the herd appeared to be stalled, seemingly forever, on the far side of the river. It appeared to be a good time to return to civilization and try his hand at something new.

He gave his notice to Finney, made one last tour of the project saying goodbye to friends with whom he had lived and worked for so long, kissed his wife and flew to Ottawa to make his final report. Elly, just a few days from term, elected to remain with Betty in Aklavik until the baby was born. Then, as soon as she could travel, the three of them would fly out by bush plane to Edmonton where Bob would join them as soon as his debriefing was completed.

The baby, a boy, arrived shortly after Bob's departure and died within a few days. He had been born without an esophagus and the facilities at the Aklavik hospital were inadequate to deal with the emergency. Elly quietly grieved the death of her son, then buried him in the stoney soil of the little graveyard on the outskirts of town. Ten days later, she and Betty flew out on a mail plane, headed for Edmonton and Bob, who had curtailed his summation in Ottawa and hurried west to be with his family when they arrived.

5

"We didn't find it there..."

EDMONTON WAS NEVER A DESTINATION. Bob was not a farmer, nor had he any desire to live in the Depression-wracked flatlands of the prairies. Soon after their reunion, they were on the move again, westward by train to Vancouver. Here, on the sound advice of the Danish consul, Bob purchased the Denman Wharf, a commercial fishing boat marina.

Their time in Vancouver was an idyllic, though brief, interlude for the young family. Bob happily spent his days puttering on the docks, yarning with the fishermen and assisting in repairs. Elly, for all the keen delight she had taken in their Arctic sojourn, was essentially a city girl and now enjoyed being back in civilization. She immediately made a number of friends among their neighbours on Denman Street. With them, she whiled away her days window-shopping, or playing bridge. The whole family enjoyed exploring the wonders of Stanley Park, the entrance to which was a mere block from their home. In addition, there was a large Scandinavian society in Vancouver that accepted them with open arms and they were popular guests at the Consulate. It was at a party in the home of the Danish consul that they met Gus Bergstrom and Einar Christiansen, the two men responsible for the next major transition in the long way around to Johnson's Crossing.

Gus, a Swede, and Einar, a Dane, had arrived in Canada in the early '30s. Meeting for the first time on the ship that brought

them to Canada, they had formed a fast friendship and together
had made the rounds of employment on the West Coast. They had
logged and fished and even tried their hand in the shipbuilding
industry, but none of this had satisfied the restlessness that had
driven them from their native lands in the first place. Now they
were both unemployed once again and seeking fresh adventure,
this time bound for the fabled goldfields of the Yukon.

All they needed was a kindred spirit, preferably one with a
bankroll with which to fund the enterprise. In Bob, they found
both spirit and cash. And as always, Elly, despite a third pregnancy,
was ready and willing to go along with anything he wanted to
do. Late in May 1935, an unlikely-looking crew of gold seekers
stepped off the train at the depot in Whitehorse: Gus, Einar and
Bob, spiffy in suits and felt hats; Elly, as smartly dressed as her
nine-month pregnancy would permit; and bright-eyed, dimpled,
four-year-old Betty.

Immediately, they got down to business, the men building
a substantial riverboat while Elly, with a minimum of fuss and

*Einar Christiansen and Gus Bergstrom, Dad's partners, work the sluice
box in Sixtymile.*

bother, produced her third child, Aksel Melvin, a nine-pound boy with a fine set of lungs and hair as yellow as the gold they would be seeking. And while all this production was going on, Betty set about charming and captivating every Indian and grizzled old prospector who lived in Whiskey Flats, the shantytown that lined the west side of the grey-green Yukon River.

˙⋅⊛⋅˙

A scant week after Aksel's birth, they were ready to go. The twenty-two-foot riverboat, sturdy and broad beamed, was loaded to the gunnels with babies and tents, pots and kettles, and in tow, a nineteen-foot canoe carrying extra food supplies, traps, bar-mining equipment and four dogs. A crowd of well-wishers gathered to help them push off and good-natured curses and advice filled the air.

"Good luck with that baby, Missus."

"Careful with that canoe, catch the current wrong you'll roll the bastard sure as hell."

"Goodbye, little girl, you find some gold, you bring some back for old John."

"Watch for the wind on Laberge, she can blow up pretty sudden. And keep right at Five Fingers, you'll be okay."

Laughing and waving, the adventurers set off, their excitement a palpable pennant flying proudly from the high prow of their boat. Gold, they had been informed, was where you found it, and by God, they were primed and ready for the search!

Their destination was an area several miles up the Big Salmon River, a major tributary to the Yukon entering a short distance below the confluence of the Teslin and Yukon rivers. It was soon after the spring breakup and all the rivers and streams were running high and swift. And so were the travellers. The mouth of the Big Salmon flashed by.

"By golly, I think that was our river!" Gus looked back in dismay. A quick consultation with the map revealed they had indeed overshot.

"What now?" asked Einar. "Shall we go back?"

The men looked uneasily at the high cutbanks. The river swept them on relentlessly, like bark on the crest of a wave, and the little outboard screamed in protest as the boiling current lifted the front of their craft and dropped out from underneath.

"I don't think I can turn her here," Bob said. The others shook their heads in agreement. "Let's go on till we can find a place to pull off, then we can decide what to do." He smiled reassuringly at his wife, who reclined on a pile of bedrolls, one arm placed lightly over Aksel, sound asleep in a wooden box beside her, the other hand clutching at the skirt of Betty's dress as she leaned perilously over the side trying to catch the spray from the bow wave. "Alright, skat?" he asked.

Elly smiled back easily. "I'm fine." And she was. A short month before, she had been living in the city, shopping and playing bridge with her friends, spending pleasant afternoons in Stanley Park with her daughter, entertaining and being entertained. Since then, she had once more packed everything in the world that they owned, bade fond adieu to new friends and had travelled a thousand miles to yet another unfamiliar corner of her adopted country. A scant three weeks later, she had given birth to her third child and was now headed for parts unknown in a runaway riverboat. She was thirty-two years old, half the world away from her mother and happy as if she were in her right mind. Elly was fine indeed.

Later, as they sat by the fire making their evening meal, it was decided that returning to Big Salmon was out of the question. The river was too high and too fast and their outboard too puny and unequal to the task.

Bob pointed to a spot on the map, a point about fifty miles upriver from Dawson. "This is the mouth of the Sixtymile River." He consulted a booklet given him by the mining recorder in Whitehorse. "It says here that they were mining in this part of the

A scant three weeks after giving birth to her third child, Elly had once more packed everything that they owned and travelled to yet another unfamiliar corner of her adopted country—but she was fine indeed.

country long before the gold rush and that quite a lot of gold was taken out. It hasn't been worked much since then." He paused and smiled. "Maybe they've been waiting for some Scandi-bloody-hoovians to come and finish the job."

Einar laughed. "Maybe they have, at that. Well, it's fine with me. Gus?"

"Yah, me as well." The three men sat, silently mulling over the latest developments. They all jumped as Elly spoke up sharply.

"Nobody has asked me what I think of this change of plan. Don't I get a vote?" She looked at them with a stern face and a cold glint in her eye.

"Yes, skat, of course you do. We just didn't think..." Bob stammered.

"No, you didn't. And I believe maybe you should. After all, I'm up to my ears in this too." She paused and looked at them severely, enjoying their discomfort.

Hesitantly, Bob asked, "Well, skat? What do you think of the Sixtymile?"

Elly made a great show of studying the map. She couldn't find the place they had been discussing but was not about to give them the satisfaction of asking. After a moment, she folded the map and put it down. "Well," she said, "since you ask..." she paused, then smiled broadly, "I think it's a great idea!"

As it turned out, it wasn't a great idea. A good idea, perhaps. Interesting, certainly. But if great is taken to mean tremendously beneficial, then it definitely was not great.

For a year they bar-mined, cleaning up little more than fair wages. Disappointed, Einar sold his share of the operation to Bob and Gus and returned to Vancouver. During the next four years, the two partners worked on the creeks in the summer, showing little for their efforts but turning a nice profit from the winter's trapping of the virgin area. To a great extent, they lived off the land, fishing for grayling, eating moose and caribou and a wide variety of wild berries, travelling to Dawson only for staples and mail. They spent one summer on a tent-raft on the Stewart River and a week on the roof of their cabin one spring when the Sixtymile over-brimmed its banks.

On that occasion, Bob and Gus had come rushing home from a supply run to Dawson, aware that the river was approaching flood stage. Bob jumped from the canoe as Gus ran it ashore and went leaping up the markedly lower bank to find his intrepid wife frantically bailing out their dirt cellar with a bucket made from a five-gallon Blazo can.

"Oh, Bob," she cried, "I've been bailing and bailing and still the water keeps coming in and everything is getting wet!"

Gently, he took the pail from her hand, explained the concept of a rising water table, and boosted their big bed onto the roof of the cabin. There, it straddled the peak and provided comfort and a ringside seat for Elly and the children as the water rose and Bob and Gus paddled in and around the camp, rescuing the dogs. They joined the family and equipment on the roof. Later, as the river continued to rise and rain threatened to compound the misery, the men erected a tent over the bed and all took shelter there to wait out nature's excesses.

They were good years, those spent on the Sixtymile, happy and relatively carefree. Gus imported his wife from the old country and Bob and Elly added two more daughters to their family. Ellen Margrethe was born in Dawson's St. Mary's Hospital, in the fall of '37 and Johanne Julie arrived on a cold January night in 1940, born on a makeshift bed in the kitchen of their cabin, Morton P.'s eldest son officiating. Mother and daughter came through in good order, but they nearly lost the midwife.

As all good things must, this period in their lives came to an end later that same year. Betty was now nine years old and, though Elly had been teaching her a rudimentary form of the three Rs, the time had come for her to enter a real school, and Aksel was ready to begin, as well. They moved to Dawson in the late part of the summer and, when school commenced, the two children were enrolled. Aksel settled easily into the grade one program and Betty, after a period of adjustment, was found to have a good foundation up to and including grade four.

Their emergence from The Bush, as they referred to their home on the Sixtymile, began an unquiet time for Bob. When they decided to leave their mining and trapping, Bob and Gus came to a parting of the ways. They had heard of work in Mayo and Gus and his wife, Signe, decided to go upriver to that town while Bob and Elly decided that Dawson would be the better place for their growing family. The two small groups journeyed together to the mouth of the Sixtymile and there, with many tears and fond farewells, they set out on separate paths, one upriver and the other, down.

Alone, Bob tried his hand at many things. He worked for most of that first winter on the gold dredges for the Yukon Consolidated Gold Company, at the princely wage of fifty-one cents per hour. After a long cold time of trying to make ends meet, he left his family in their rented home in town and returned to the Sixtymile for the spring muskrat season. The conversion of the rat harvest into cash carried them through the summer while Bob again worked for YCGC. A part-time job in a local laundry gave Elly an outlet for her restless energy. She also quickly got

Betty (holding Ellen and Polly the dog) was now nine years old, and the time had come for her to enter a real school.

They were good years in Sixtymile, and two daughters were added to the family, Ellen Margrethe in 1937 and Johanne Julie in 1940.

involved in the Anglican Women's Auxiliary and the Imperial Order of Daughters of the Empire. These were war years and the ladies were busy sewing and knitting for the armed forces. That winter, Bob got caught up in the war effort in quite another way.

It was the winter of '42 and the Alaska Highway was being built to facilitate the buildup of military defences in Alaska. Japanese attacks on the Aleutian Panhandle had caught the Alaska Defence Command with its drawers at half-mast, and red-faced officials set about remedying the situation with tremendous Sturm und Drang. Some of the Sturm enveloped a group of Dawson men, Bob included. They were hired to help build a string of air bases, a major part of the defence infrastructure. The wages were excellent but it was a bitterly cold winter and Bob spent most of it at Snag, where the temperature dipped into the minus seventies and took up residence there for weeks on end. He was pleased to be working at the well-paying job and enjoyed the camaraderie of the men but he missed his family, as is evidenced in this little ballad he wrote for the occasion of Elly's fortieth birthday, which she spent alone in Dawson.

Trapping in the virgin area near Sixtymile yielded a large lynx harvest in 1938.

"Spring on the Sixtymile"

Yes, this is the time of the season
The robin begins to sing,
Back on the Sixtymile River,
With bluebirds and swallows and spring.

When the geese and the cranes go zooming
And screeching away—they are gone—
To the North; to the shores of the Arctic,
The home of the midnight sun.

Where birches and aspen poplars
Turn green overnight on the hills,
Each light little breeze, your nostrils
With the odor of balsam fills.

I remember the times of the breakup,
When the river's song rose to a roar,
To nature's mighty crescendo
This year, as each year before.

And the youngsters would play where the snowbank
Had left but a pool at the trail,
With one of my moccasin rubbers
And an N.C. bill for a sail.

And you, little woman of Sixty,
Would greet me each night with a smile,
When coming home from the hunting
From way up the Sixtymile,

Would sit with me out in the garden,
Quiet, watching the set of the sun,
With its gold and its silver and purple,

Or a shooting star on its run.

Oh, I long for my Sixtymile River
And the woman—my only one;
For my sweet little darling of forty
And the woman of Sixty, are one.

Bob came home for a brief holiday at Christmas but when he returned again in May, it was with a spring in his step and brand new marching orders for all.

"We're moving to Whitehorse with the first boat upriver!" Belatedly, he took his wife in his arms and kissed her soundly, grinning down at her. "Unless, of course, you'd prefer to wait here while I go by myself." But Elly had a firm grip on her man once again and there would be no running off without them this time. When the *Aksala* sailed on June 3, 1943, it was with the entire Porsild family, bag and baggage.

For all of that summer and most of the next winter, Bob worked with Ole Wickstrom, cutting and hauling wood into Whitehorse. A bout with double pneumonia in March brought his participation in this enterprise to an abrupt halt. Weak and debilitated, he spent several months recuperating. To keep his spirits up and some cash flowing into the family coffers, he undertook the building of several boats. It was pleasant work, which could be accomplished as he felt up to it and allowed him to spend time with his wife and children, a pleasure he had had to forgo too often in the recent past. The interlude was short-lived. Once again the war came close, albeit in a roundabout way. This time, the offer of employment was on the Canol (Canadian Oil) Project. Again, Bob went away to work, carpenter tools in hand, leaving a disappointed Elly to cope with life on the home front. She did, of course, with her usual style and grace.

Once more, she went to work in a laundry, joined several women's groups, and her rich soprano was a welcome addition to the choir at the Anglican Log Church. Before long, Betty and Aksel had added their voices to the junior choir. When Bob

Bob poses on the Yukon Winter Carnival float in 1945. After their emergence from The Bush, life in Whitehorse was an unquiet time for the family.

returned from the Canol, he found his little group well settled into the fabric of the community, his three oldest children in school and his wife gainfully employed.

There was not a lot of employment in Whitehorse that winter but Bob kept busy, first building a bell tower for the Log Church and later, odd-job carpentering around town. Then, in the summer of '45, came the first of three jobs that would point him down the road to Johnson's Crossing. In June, he undertook to build a cabin cruiser for Mike Nolan, an ex-Mountie with great plans for a fishing resort at Marsh Lake, about thirty-five miles southeast of Whitehorse, and the following spring he accepted a contract to build a two-storey log hotel at Burwash Landing on Kluane Lake, about a hundred and seventy-five miles in the other direction.

As always, Elly was resigned to remaining behind, but Bob had been absent from his family just too many times. Enough was enough! They would all go. Besides, there was work for everyone. On the cruiser job, there was firewood to be gathered to feed the fire under the steamer—a long piece of heavy pipe in which the bones of the boat were softened before being shaped

In June, Bob undertook to build a cabin cruiser at Marsh Lake, the first of three jobs that would bring him down the road to Johnson's Crossing.

and curved into ribs. And extra hands were needed to set clamps and hold the oak boards steady and fetch and carry. Even chubby little paws could, as required, bring a cool drink of "bug juice," a raspberry-flavoured drink so-called because of the many blackfly corpses that ended up in the sweet residue.

There was less for the younger members to do the following summer at Burwash, but Elly, already an expert with the draw-knife from their cabin-building days in The Bush, was pressed into service peeling the hundreds of logs required for the forty-by-sixty-foot building. And she could not have been happier. Hair covered by an old bandana and stylish in a pair of Bob's old bib overalls, the legs turned up to accommodate her shorter shanks, she worked at her husband's side. Humming and singing, her strong arms moved rhythmically, stripping long curls of bark from the green logs. Slowly, round by round, the great building rose and by summer's end, the glistening yellow walls were up, rising eighteen feet above the ground, ready for the huge timbers that would support the massive roof.

But once again the spectre of separation loomed large. One

evening, they strolled along a pebble beach where the clear water of Kluane lapped gently, uncharacteristically calm. The next day, Elly and the children would be returning to the reality of Whitehorse. School would be resuming and Elly had promised Kai Gertsen that she would be back at her pressing machine by September 1.

"I don't want to go back without you." She didn't look at Bob but kept her gaze on the edge of the beach where the minute waves dappled and splintered, flashing back the fading tints of a flame-red sunset. "The kids could go to school here and I could help you…" She paused and raised her eyes as Bob clasped her shoulders in his big hands and turned her to him.

"No, you cannot." He spoke gently, but decisively. "It will soon be too cold to stay in the big tent and the lodge isn't finished enough for us to live there. Besides, it will only be till Christmas, then I'll be home again."

Famous last words. Well, he did come home for Christmas but it was to be a full eight months before he was finished with his contract at Burwash. Most of his work was inside, fortunately, because this was the notorious winter of '46, when new record-breaking low temperatures were set all over the North: minus eighty-three Fahrenheit in Snag, minus seventy-two in Whitehorse. To keep his work area comfortable, Bob simply partitioned off the part of the building in which he was working and moved his barrel stove from place to place. Besides, after the long years he had spent in preparation for the reindeer drive and later bar-mining and trapping, this indoor work was a snap.

The extremely cold weather, however, did create problems for Elly. Their rented log house in Whitehorse was old and drafty, especially the kitchen, which had been added on without a whole lot of care and attention. No matter how she filled the big wood heater in the front room or how carefully she set damper and draft before leaving for work in the morning, by noon the stove was always empty and the house like a tomb. Similarly, Elly was up several times during the night to stoke the fire but even so, by morning everyone would be crowded

Once again the spectre of separation loomed large as Elly and the children returned to the reality of Whitehorse.

into one bed for warmth. The bitter cold seemed to crouch in all the corners waiting for the fire to dwindle, allowing it to creep under the covers at the foot of a bed, nibbling at small toes and bare shins as it advanced.

In the morning Elly would leap out of bed and stoke the heater, kindle a blaze in the kitchen cookstove and put on the kettle and a pot of oatmeal prepared the night before. Returning to her crowded nest, she would huddle close and teasingly lay cold hands and feet on squirming small bodies until, laughing and protesting, all would be awake.

At 7:45, Elly would leave for work, dressed like an Eskimo against the seven-block walk in the snapping cold. Soon after, Betty would oversee the departure of the younger children to the big, square, white-and-green Lambert Street School, a mere half block from their home. She would then tuck one last log into the heater, fill the firebox in the kitchen range and get herself off to high school, a long cold walk to the far end of town. Frostbite was the order of the day. Half a block or half a town to travel, they all bore the flaming marks of winter's vicious pinch.

Lunch was always a fiasco. It was decided that Betty should take a sandwich with her; it was just too far for her to return at noon especially when it was so cold. The responsibility for preparing lunch therefore fell to Ellen and Aksel. Their intentions were good and with a minimum of dawdling they would hurry home at noon. Aksel would light the fire in the cookstove, carefully building up the kindling over the crumpled newspaper, as he had been taught. If he left the lid off a little longer than necessary and allowed the flame and smoke to billow out into the room, in a gentle touch of pyromania, it later went unremarked in the general confusion of lunch-getting. When the fire was well and truly lit, together they would lift the large soup pot from its cold storage on the floor by the kitchen door and put it on the stove. Then, once again, they would put on mittens and boots (jackets had not been removed, the temperature within the house being not much warmer than without) and trudge up to Pinchin's Bakery for a loaf of fresh bread. By the time Elly got home, lunch, as such, was ready.

The soup, an enormous potful to last the week and placed immediately over the business end of Aksel's brisk, hot fire, day after day, was always stuck on the bottom and little scorched peas or lentils imparted an acrid flavour to the thick rich brew. By Friday, the remaining soup was all but inedible by virtue of having its lowest layer overheated just one time too many.

In addition to the soup, they dined on slices of fresh bread spread liberally with butter and jam. Of course, one would be hard-pressed to describe as slices the hunks of dough that were hacked from the compressed lump that had begun life as a crusty round loaf in the oven at Pinchin's Bakery, lived its short span clamped under a chubby arm rendered unfeeling by several thick layers of flannel and wool, and died without a hint of struggle under the serrated edge of a dull bread knife in the sooty, drafty Porsild kitchen. No, slices they were not. But as Aksel would later recall, "They sure did hold a lot of butter." They did too, great slabs of it carved from a brick as hard as any nugget they ever found on the Sixtymile, and the bread and butter made a solid platform for the dollops of glossy red preserves heaped on to take the curse from the burnt soup.

They say that time dulls the memory and perhaps the numbing temperatures had something to do with it too, but those lunches are remembered with great pleasure and satisfaction by all. In fact, most of the memories of that time are good. The cold was an enemy, endured, resisted and eventually forced into retreat with the kindly assistance of the strengthening rays of the spring sun. Patches of frostbite faded beneath freckles that popped like tiny brown kernels of corn, and pea soup that had no little black things floating on the surface just didn't taste right somehow. And above all was the gut-tingling anticipation of the end of the Burwash job.

As spring began liberating the countryside from its prison of snow and ice, the sap began to rise in more than the trees. Bob, with the scent of homecoming in his nostrils, sat down and poured out his eagerness in the following poem:

> There is spring in the air
> And of swallows, a pair;
> The robin, he sings of his love.
> Each morning he sits on the top of a tree
> And fills the blue sky with his twittering glee.
> And my heart with a radiant smile.
>
> Robin sings to his mate
> In a bush, by the gate;
> She lies on the nest all the day.
> I join in his glee and I sing love's old song,
> To my mate back at home, where I dream, where I long,
> While I toil, and I work with a smile.
>
> Do you hear all my trills
> Rolling down from the hills?
> Little darling, to tell you once more;

You fill all my heart of each spring, of each day,
With the hope and the joy, ever young, ever gay,
"Twi-di-wit! Twi-di-wit!"—with a smile!

Elly smiled fondly at the image of her big ruddy husband in duet with a red-breasted *"pippe-nakker"* and laid the sentimental offering away in her cedar jewel box. Gruff he was, and bad-tempered and impatient sometimes, but a more loving husband and father would be hard to find. The growing pile of billets-doux was testimony to that love, but right now Elly had no time to linger over Bob's poetic renderings. A note accompanying the trills and twittering foretold a new contract and yet another uprooting. Once again there were arrangements to be made and packing to be done.

The Department of Indian Affairs was planning to build a new residential school at Fox Point, a lovely little jut of land on Teslin Lake, close to the settlement of Teslin. They had purchased two old US Army buildings at Johnson's Crossing and could Bob please go now and, for slight consideration, dismantle those and oversee their removal to the Point? Well, of course Bob could. And would. The Burwash job was coming to an end.

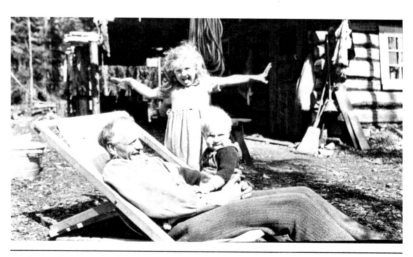

Bob, with Betty and Aksel in Sixtymile: a more loving husband and father would be hard to find.

6

"A place in the summer sun..."

"HE'S HERE!" THE FRONT DOOR opened and Aksel skidded into the front room followed closely by a tall, slim man with greying dark hair. "Hello, Bob, sorry I'm late. It took me a little longer than I figured to get ready."

Dad shook his head. "It doesn't matter, Ken. We don't plan on doing more than just get moved today. It looks like rain, too. Do you have a big tarp?" As he spoke, the two men went outside to begin loading the heap of bags and boxes that filled the sidewalk beside our house on Lambert Street. Dad had hired Ken Pryor, a Whitehorse-based trucker he'd met at Burwash, to move our belongings to the new temporary summer home at Johnson's Crossing. It was getting to be old hat, this camping out every summer, but the pile of equipment and provisions never got smaller. Ken's big red truck was filled to the top of the side-racks by the time we got under way, Mom and Dad riding in front with Ken, we kids and Jiggs under the tarpaulin in the back. We played and dozed and sang and generally managed to entertain ourselves for what seemed like hours. Suddenly, there was a rapping on the back window and we roused to feel the truck slowing and then stopping. Being under the tarp, we had missed seeing the neat camp on the west bank of the Teslin River and the smooth concrete of the long bridge had slipped under us without remark, but now we piled out of the truck into the centre of another, smaller camp and stood looking around. We didn't want to miss anything else.

The Canol Road, slightly over five hundred miles of narrow, bumpy cow trail, was built to provide access to the oil fields at Norman Wells in the Northwest Territories. Conceived by the US War Department (and, I presume, born of the virgin wilderness) to help fuel Alaska and protect it from a Japanese invasion, the road and a four-inch-diameter pipeline were constructed from Norman Wells, through MacMillan Pass and Ross River, to Johnson's Crossing. From there, the pipeline carried the oil to a refinery in Whitehorse.

The Canol Project, begun in 1942 and completed in 1944, included the road and pipeline, the refinery, airfields and telephone line, as well as camps, pumping stations and tank farms. Only about a million barrels of oil were pumped to the refinery before the war ended in 1945 and the $130-million project was abandoned.

Whole camps, pumping stations and truck and supply depots were simply locked up and vacated. Machinery ground to a halt and was left sitting in its tracks. There was some attempt, on the part of individuals, to hide or otherwise camouflage stores and equipment. For years rumours abounded of "...a whole pile of Canol pipe. Must be six or seven acres of it... yeah, and two D-6 Cats, yup, right in the lake, just twenty feet from the shore... and a ten-kilowatt power plant in the gravel pit... mutter, mutter..." Everyone knew someone who knew someone else who had seen, with his own two eyes, a whole fleet of trucks parked in a clearing, not two hundred feet from the road. But in 1947, except for minor inroads made by local freebooters, the Canol was still more or less complete, as was the orderly and empty installation in which Dad was to tear down the two buildings for Indian Affairs.

The installation was actually in two parts: the base camp of the Canol Road, spread over twenty acres at its immediate junction with the Alaska Highway, and a quarter of a mile south a telephone relay station consisting of a mess hall, repeater station and several barrack buildings. It was to the relay station that we came.

"Many thanks, Ken," Dad said as the two men unloaded the last few pieces. "We'll look for you in about three weeks to move the first load down to Fox Point."

"Sure Bob, just give me a holler when you're ready. Good-bye, Mrs. Porsild. See yuh, kids." He gave Jo a special smile as she stood there with Jiggs hugged tight in her arms. "You be a good girl, squirt."

We stood waving as Ken expertly swung the battered old truck over the windrow and onto the highway. As he vanished in a choking cloud of dust and exhaust, we turned back to the camp.

Immediately, Dad and Aksel set off to reconnoitre the two structures slated for demolition while Mom and the rest of us selected living quarters. We had plenty to choose from.

Excluding the mess hall and the repeater station, both of which were marked for sacrifice on the altar of Indian Affairs' segregation policies, there were eight of the drab, prefabricated Butler huts and several frame sheds. My mother chose the barracks closest to the mess hall for our home away from home, reasoning that for the time being, anyway, the kitchen area of the hall could be utilized in the way it was intended. When Dad and Ax returned, they found us hard at work setting up our sleeping arrangements. With the usual amount of bickering, spaces were favoured and selected.

"I'm the oldest and should have the place nearest the door." That was Betty, exercising her prerogative. "Well, I'm not sleeping beside Aksel. He snores and besides, his feet..."

Although Mom was usually quick to bring a bit of perspective to our wrangling ("Would anyone like to go to bed? Now? Without supper?"), on this occasion she simply left us to thrash out the floor plan and exited through the door at the far end. Without a referee, our pecking order soon asserted itself. Our mattresses and sleeping bags were laid out in an orderly fashion, from Betty's, by the door, to Johanne's pallet beside Mom and Dad's bed. Storing our few personal possessions in the territory allotted to us, we left Betty to the tireless arranging and re-arranging of her toilet articles and went outside to join our parents by the mess hall. As they slowly walked around the large building, planning their attack, we trooped along behind, waiting for a lull in their conversation.

"Dad," Ax said. "Dad, can we go exploring?"

They stopped and Dad's pale blue eyes rested on each of us in turn. "Have you finished making up your beds?" he asked.

"Yes, Daddy."

"Alright, you can go." As one, we wheeled to sprint away. "But don't go on the bridge," he added.

"No, Dad, we won't." We left then to make a detailed circuit of the area.

Neat streets, narrow but well-gravelled, divided the camp into orderly segments and where nature had begun to reclaim her own, wild strawberries grew in profusion around the buildings, and great clumps of fireweed, just beginning to bloom, grew in every open space. Little white poplar shrubs were springing up all over, even in the beaten path we now followed bordering the north-perimeter relay station. Here we stopped, transfixed.

Before us stretched a wide-open space, sort of a no man's land between the two encampments. It was featureless except for an immense, red-rusted storage tank at the back of the clearing. On the far side, we could see three or four long, high garages, set broadside to our view. But it was neither the tank nor the camp that caused us to stop and stare, our hearts thumping a little in surprise and excitement. It was the smoke coming from the chimney of a bungalow just at the entrance to the camp. And the greenish-brown vehicle just pulling away from it, headed in our direction. We turned and ran, whooping, back to home base.

"Daddy, Daddy, there's people living over there, we saw some smoke and a car and they're coming..." Our voices ran down as the old US Army carryall rounded the end of the station and pulled up before us with a scattering of dust and gravel. The door opened and out stepped a heavy-set man of forty or so, full-faced, with a speckled, bristly little mustache. He held out his hand to Dad. "You must be Porsild. I was told to expect you."

My father shook the proffered hand. "Yes," he said, genially, "I'm Bob Porsild and this is my wife, Elly." Mom held out her hand, in turn, and the stocky man pressed it briefly and introduced himself. "Morris, is my name. Jack. I'm the representative of the US Army, here."

Well, that was gilding the lily just a trifle, on his part. In actual fact, Jack Morris was the caretaker of three pump stations on the Alaska Highway: the one here at JC, one a few miles south of Teslin and another about fifteen miles toward Whitehorse. His duties consisted of bi-weekly trips to each of these and monthly reports on any vandalism or changes to the status quo. It was a well-paying, cushy job, requiring no great skill or energy, and Jack, a good-hearted, friendly man rarely stimulated into excessive bursts of ambition, was perfect for the job. Somewhat given to delusions of grandeur and with an over-inflated idea of his importance in the general scheme of things, he was something of an enigma: shy in the presence of women and completely baffled by children, his own included. He turned now to those, seated in the vehicle. "What are you doing, still sitting there? Come and meet these kids." He looked at Dad. "Kids, darned if I can figger 'em. They've been after me all morning to come here and now they just sit like lumps. Come on, you guys, and say hello. This is Dick," he pointed to a chubby, good-looking boy of ten. "And this is Bud." Dick ducked his head shyly, looking at the ground, but Bud, all straw-coloured hair and freckles, grinned sunnily, showing wide-open gaps where new broad teeth were just starting to grow.

Mom motioned us forward with a wave of her arm. "This is Aksel. And Ellen and Johanne." She looked around vaguely. "We have an older daughter, Betty, but I'm not sure where she is." We all smiled at each other, scuffling our feet.

"Irene—Irene's the wife—and I have a daughter too." Jack's face lit with pride. "Barbara. She's two and can spell her own name." He stopped, embarrassed. "Well, I should be getting back,

Once again, the family was united. From left to right: Bob, Aksel, Jo, Elly, Ellen and Betty.

I'll bring the Missus over when you're all settled." He squeezed under the wheel of the narrow carryall. "You comin', you guys?"

"Could they stay for a while, Mr. Morris?" Johanne's small face turned up to his.

"Well, I guess they could." He scratched a mole on his cheek with a thumbnail, his mouth opened slightly to stretch the skin. "Don't get underfoot," he told them. "And be home in time for supper or there'll be trouble." Saluting with forefinger to forelock, he ground the starter to a roaring crescendo and belted off, leaving us in a billow of river-silt particles.

Dick and Buddy were eager and indefatigable tour guides and by late afternoon we'd had a complete look at Johnson's Crossing. From a removable panelled wall in one of the office buildings, to the top of the storage tank, to a warehouse crammed full of every size of tire imaginable, we'd seen it all, including a private viewing of some fairly intense passion exhibited by their pair of Mackenzie huskies, Punch and Judy.

"See that?" asked Bud, in a nonchalant tone. "They're in heat. Copulating, that's what my mom says, and pretty soon we're gonna have a bunch of puppies. And you can have as many as you want 'cause old Jude has them all the time."

"Hey, you kids get outta there, leave them dogs alone!"

We peered around the corner of the house to see Jack Morris tinkering with the innards of the carryall. The way he drove necessitated a lot of tinkering, we came to find out. He threw back his head and yelled again. "Dammit, Dick, get away from there!"

Behind him, the screen door opened and Irene Morris came out. At least we assumed it was Jack's wife. Barely topping five feet in her high heels, she was an exquisitely feminine little person, black curly hair, long-lashed sleepy dark eyes and a tidy, curvy body all wrapped in a crisp red and white polka-dotted dress.

"Hi there, kids," she said, smiling easily. "Whatcha doing? Come and meet Barbara."

We visited a while longer with the Morris family, playing with the boys and their sister, a carbon copy in miniature of her mother. Then Irene called her men in to wash up for supper, so we saddled up and headed out, promising to return in the morning.

Later, during a lull in conversation, Jo dropped a pebble into the pool of small supper sounds. "Daddy, can we have some puppies?"

"Puppies? Where are you going to get puppies from?"

"From Dick and Buddy. Punch and Judy are in heat and today they were co-operating and Bud says they do it all the time and we can have all we want," she finished triumphantly.

We couldn't have all we wanted, as it turned out. We couldn't even have one. "We have Jiggs," Dad said, affectionately scratching the old tom's ragged ears. "That's enough." He got up from the table, leaned down and kissed Mom on the cheek. "*Tak for mad*, skat. Leave the dishes for now, let's go and see how to get some water."

Getting water would always be a problem in Johnson's Crossing. That summer, we lived high above the river and had no vehicle to get around in. Aksel clambered down the steep clay bluffs to get our first few bucketfuls, but the way was long and hazardous. The alternative was to take the long river road that curved down the east bank to fetch up under the bridge. It was easier walking but infinitely longer and got more so as the pails gained weight on the return trip. On this evening, we were going to try something new and we went down the highway to the bridge with the buckets and a long rope.

Walking out to the middle span, Dad tied a pail to the rope and tossed it over to the river below. He jiggled the pail till it tipped and filled, then hauled it, hand over hand, up to the bridge. It worked but was not very efficient, as only Dad had the strength to accomplish the feat.

Jack Morris solved the problem when he pulled up the next day with a tanker of water he had hauled from the pumphouse at the Brook's Brook maintenance camp. "I bring water home every few days; I'll fill your buckets if you want." He went on to describe the trouble the US Army had had there, drilling a dozen or more wells through the endless, impervious river silt to a depth of several hundred feet without success. "Oh yeah, they drilled them wells all over the place, one right down on the shore of the river. And dry as dust. They ended up pumping the goddam stuff up and over the bank." Jack spat reflectively and thumbnailed his mole. "Guess if the whole damn US Army couldn't get water, we sure won't, eh? Well, better get home, the Missus wants to wash clothes." And he was gone with a roar.

Once Jack provided the answer to the water question, we were home free and ready to get on with our summer.

Once again, the family was united and though we didn't know it at the time, it was to be the last free gypsy-summer we would spend together. Not the last summer when we could all be together; in fact, our altogetherness would never again be at risk. But it was the last time that we would ever be able to pick up and go, as a family, wherever and whenever we chose. Only the timetable of the contract could cramp our style and as long as the lumber was at Fox Point by September 1, how or when it got there were not important. So, we picnicked and swam, gathered berries, climbed mountains, and explored and played. But first, we worked. All of us.

Perhaps not so much expertise is required for the demolition of a building as constructing one, but certainly the energy demanded must be nearly equal. We rose early every morning and as we washed ourselves and tidied the barracks, Mom would prepare a huge pot of mush. Beaming and humming, brimming with good-wifery, she would feed us and send us on our way, some of us later than sooner. (There was no knothole for me during that time and some days I was hard-pressed to dispose of the foul stuff and ended up having to eat it most of the time.) Once the dishes were washed, the soup kettle replaced the porridge pot, the fire in the stove was banked low and slow, and Mom would hurry off, hammer in hand, to pull nails and pile lumber until it was time to make lunch.

We kids helped where we were needed, fetching and carrying the bug juice and 6-12 mosquito repellent, the claw-bar that had been left at the other side of the mess hall, or the nail-puller that had fallen down and was hiding in the strawberries and young poplar. We sorted boards and piled them, picked up nails and collected trash. We got in the way and underfoot. Finally, we would be released to go and play and we'd head over to the big camp, picking up the Morris boys on the way.

Dick and Bud added much to our adventures. Not that we needed a whole lot more inspiration than the Canol scenario: deserted buildings, many of them chockablock with equipment and filing cabinets full of papers and stationery and office para-phernalia; the big kitchens with galvanized sinks and big rusty wood ranges; the complete garages. They all supplied more grist for our adventure mills than we could properly utilize in several summers. Outside, rows of wanigans, small shelters mounted on tracks, forecast no end of experiences on the Oregon Trail, and the discovery of an attached steel ladder to the top of the thirty-foot fuel storage tank signalled hi-jinks in high places. Of course, the latter escapade was one of the first and most emphatic of parental no-nos, ranking right up there with breaking windows and walking on the handrail of the bridge. "Don't let me catch you climbing on the tank!" And naturally, being good and obedient children, we didn't... let him catch us. Dad's admonition took the fine edge of enjoyment from the tank. A kid should never have to strain to hear the echo of a whisper; it does something unnatural to the spirit! But we could never risk bellowing down into the depths; Dad could be pretty unreasonable when roused to anger. The rousing was not all that difficult, either. So, after tempting fate and our father's ire a few times, we unanimously decided that it wasn't worth the wear and tear on the nerves and wrote the tank out of our dramas.

The bridge was something else again. In the first place, it was out of sight, out of earshot and the only constraint was that we not walk on the handrail. Second, it had everything in the world we could possibly wish for. The decking, seventeen hundred feet of perfectly smooth, almost level concrete for running, biking or playing hopscotch, was bordered on both sides by sidewalks. These were eight inches high and about sixteen wide, well designed for walking or sitting or kneeling on to lean out over the guardrail to spit into the river. We did a lot of spitting, working up as much moisture as we could and then opening our lips to allow the blob to slip gently out, disintegrating and disappearing from our sight, almost instantly. Over and over we'd do it, until at last we were bone dry, spit right out.

Above the walkways—actually, they were bumpers, I believe, but always referred to by us as sidewalks—were the wooden handrails, white-painted and smooth as satin to the touch. This railing was square cut from Douglas fir and bolted to uprights every five feet. The upper surface of the rail was about six inches wide, oodles of room to accommodate rubbersoled sneakers for the forbidden, death-defying walks out over the valley floor nearly a hundred feet below.

Under the decking was a framework of steel girders, as complex and alluring as any playground jungle gym, for climbing on and hanging from and otherwise impressing your peers with your bravery and derring-do. And when you tired of that or when your trembling knees and sweat-slick hands refused to further aid and abet your foolishness, there were always the great, hitherto unblemished spaces of grey-blue steel for writing on with crayons or, preferably, chalk. I should probably tell you here that though we were extremely well-behaved, well-brought-up children, where chalk was concerned, there was a streak of larceny, pure wool and a yard wide, running through each of us. At no time during our childhood can I ever remember not having an abundance of the stuff, pilfered, no doubt, during at-the-board exercises and smuggled home in our lunch box. And it was perfect for the pictures and messages we inscribed with talent and imagination on the huge steel chalkboards: "Richard Thomas Allen Morris" and "I love W.P." (that one in small letters in an unobtrusive corner, its authorship vehemently denied when discovered) and "Dickie is a jerk!" signed with tremendous satisfaction and gusto, "Bud."

But the most marvellous thing about the bridge was a 1942 American copper, sunk into the concrete and flush with the surface, about a hundred feet from its western abutment. Like a magnet, it drew us and regardless what our original reason for going to the bridge, our ultimate destination was always The Penny. Around it we'd sit like ragtag gypsies, picking and scratching at the coin in its grey stone setting, attempting to effect its liberation, theorizing on its origin and speculating on its probably mystical-magical properties. "Everybody, make a wish." And we'd close our eyes tightly and screw up our faces and after a while peer through slitted lids to see if anyone was still at it, not wanting to disturb a serious desire before it had been fully expressed. By summer's end, I was fairly sure the coin had no special powers. I was still a girl and Mom was still refusing to buy me overalls like Aksel's.

The camp on the west bank held little fascination for us. There was not much there that could not be had, doubled in spades, in the big camp. But there were two features on the west bank that added much to our days. One was a lazy little creek that meandered down from the hills behind the valley to enter the river a hundred yards above the bridge and the other was a big old barge that had ferried men and equipment from one side of the river to the other during construction days.

By the end of August, we had either floated leisurely or pitched recklessly down every major river we could think of, and had sailed all the seven seas, to boot. We were, by turn, pirates and rum-runners and Mississippi rivermen. We were sailors on a battleship. And, when that palled, we took to the air as pilots on an aircraft carrier, taking off and returning in varying stages of disrepair from having encountered "Zeroes at five o'clock, sir!" We always managed to dispatch the enemy but not before they had managed to get in a few hits of their own. Sweaty with exertion and licking our wounds, we'd jump from the barge and head for the creek to cool off in the clear shallow water at the delta.

Two Native families shared temporary residence with us that year, although "temporary" is not quite accurate. Joe and Kate Henry were in the process of moving from their long-time home on an island twelve miles downriver to a new log house that Joe and his sons had built just below the bridge. They had lived at Big Island since the early '30s, fishing and trapping and selling fresh vegetables from their garden to the paddlewheelers that came up the river to trade in Teslin. Now the construction of the Alaska Highway had ended the era of the big boats and the Henrys were moving closer to civilization.

The other family, Jake and Mary Jackson, actually lived at Jackson's Point, an attractive deep cove cradled in the protective arm of a broad sand spit, just a mile down lake from Brook's Brook. Like the Henrys, they spent their year hunting and trapping, but in August when the king salmon were running they moved to their fish camp on the willow point beside our swimming hole at the mouth of the creek. We saw little of the Henrys during our stay, but Jake and Mary's daughters, shy, pretty girls in their late teens, often joined us swimming and "Auntie" Mary made us welcome in their tent camp.

"Hello, kids," she would say, her wide brown face shining with pleasure. "Come. Sit down, have tea. Johnnie, get logs! Dorothy..." She gestured broadly and Dorothy immediately began measuring tea leaves into the blackened tea-billy that hung over the open fire. Johnnie, a tall, good-humoured man in his thirties, hastened to carry out his mother's order and brought cut logs for us to sit upon. Cups of sweet black tea would be handed round, or dishes of soapberry ice cream, a bittersweet froth made by beating ripened soapberries with a little water and a lot of sugar, and afterwards, Jake, a taciturn but kindly man, would take up an unfinished snowshoe and demonstrate his art.

We were rapt students of his wordless demonstrations as he steamed thin birch sticks, softening the wood so that it might be curved into the required shape. The frames were wired, toe and tail, and holes were drilled exactly two gnarled finger-widths apart all around the frame. Babiche, string cut from rawhide and stretched and scraped to sinewy toughness, was then threaded through the holes and woven to fill in the shoe.

The pattern of weaving of the Teslin snowshoe is quite distinctive and easily identified. "Like ptarmigan tracks." Johnnie directed our attention to the open criss-cross design. "We have snowshoes for a long time but just frames. Don't work so good." The wrinkles at the corners of his eyes deepened as he mimed a hunter on webless shoes floundering in heavy snow. Even Jake ceased his task and we all watched intently as Johnnie lifted his knees nearly to his chest trying to get through the tall drifts. Suddenly, his hand went to his forehead, shading his eyes. "Out of bush walk little bird with feathers on his feet. 'You don't travel well,' say the bird. 'Why you don't walk on top of snow like me?' 'My shoes sink every time,' say the hunter. 'I cannot walk on top and I can't catch rabbits.'" Johnnie's expressive face showed the hunter's anguish at his failure to provide food for his people. "So the little bird ran back and forth, back and forth in front of the hunter, then he say, 'Look on my path. Take babiche, fill shoes with tracks. You walk like ptarmigan!' And the hunter do it and oh golly, pretty soon he walk on top of drift, get many rabbits."

We clapped our hands in relief of the tense situation and in appreciation of Johnnie's entertainment. Auntie Mary poured more tea and we watched with renewed interest as Jake went on with his intricate weaving, obedient to the ptarmigan's instructions. Much later, we would take our leave and, on the way home, stop at the copper for another wish. "Please, when I open my eyes, I want to be an Indian and live in a tent and walk on snowshoes." Opening my un-Indian blue eyes, I would check out my pale un-Indian skin and sigh. Nope, no special powers at all!

It was a wonderful summer and too soon the first frosts were turning the tender leaves on the young poplars to pale gold and making it difficult to get out of bed in the morning in our unheated barracks. The buildings had been levelled, their sites cleared and only the outlining poplar and strawberry plants were left to show they'd ever been. Ken Pryor was expected momentarily, to take the last load of material to Fox Point, after which he would pick us up and return us to our home on Lambert Street in Whitehorse.

With regret, we said goodbye to our new friends. "We'll miss you." Little did we know that it would only be a matter of a few weeks before we'd be standing on the bridge hollering "Good night!" to the boys before retiring in another new bedroom, this time in a low, rounded Quonset hut.

7

"Use your imagination..."

"C'MON, ELLEN, EVERYONE ELSE is up!" My eyes flew open and I stared, disoriented, at the unfamiliar arched ceiling above my bed.

"What?" I turned my head to see Aksel skinning into his overalls.

"C'mon," he said again. "It's morning and Dad's making pancakes. I can hear him singing." He headed for the door.

"Wait!" I cried, jumping out of bed as I remembered we were back at JC. "I'm coming." But he had already gone.

I pulled the long flannelette nightgown over my head, wincing as the chill morning air ruffled my bare skin, raising goosebumps. Last night, as I had divested myself of my clothes, my mother had neatly folded and piled them on the foot of my bed; now they lay in an untidy heap on the floor, kicked off during a vigorous enactment of subconscious activities. I picked them up and began a reversal of last night's removal.

Cotton underpants. Rib-knit undershirt, an old one of Aksel's, snug now, even on me, and soon destined for a duster judging by the lacy look of its hem. Over that, a grey flannel vest with long dangling garters. A white rayon slip. And over all, a practical brown cotton dress patterned with small red and yellow flowers. It was high-necked with a round white collar, gathered at the waist and cinched tightly around my sturdy body with two long strips of material attached at the side seam and tied in a bow at the back. I hauled on the strings and knotted the bow as tightly as I could; the darn thing was always coming undone! I brushed my hands down the front of my dress. It looked pretty grubby, wrinkled and stained from yesterday's adventures. Oh well.

I reached for the long, brown cotton stockings and stood with them in my hand for a moment. How I hated them! Ribbed and formless, they hung on my legs like wrinkled tubes, corrugated at the knee and ankle no matter how tightly I pulled them up, and gaping down below my hemline in uneven scallops despite the carefully set metal garters. Not today, I decided, thrusting the offensive hose under my pillow. I grabbed up my long-sleeved sweater and ran out, pulling it on as I went.

Johanne met me at the door as I emerged. "Hi, Ellen," she said brightly. "Daddy says get washed, the pancakes are ready." We hurried over to the makeshift cook shack where Dad presided over the traditional Sunday ceremony.

"Morning, Mum," I said, kissing her cheek. "Morning, Daddy." He leaned his bristly cheek down for my hasty smack. My mother surveyed my rather bedraggled appearance.

"Where are your stockings?"

"I didn't have time..." I began.

"After breakfast you make time," she said, matter-of-factly. She unravelled my braids, picked up a brush and began to groom the thick mane of waist-length hair, over and over until each blonde strand lay smooth and slick. After exchanging the brush for a heavy comb, and lining that up with my nose, she bisected my head evenly and with the ease born of long practice, twined each hank into a pigtail and handed me the ends to hold. She took up the crumpled red ribbons that had adorned yesterday's braids, dipped them briefly into the wash basin, stepped close to the stove where Dad was scraping the last of the batter into a frying pan, and expertly ironed them on the abbreviated tin chimney.

"There," she said, tying the second bow. She stood back, looked at me critically and adjusted the alignment of the heavy plaits as they fell over my shoulders. "Good as new. Get washed now. Breakfast's ready."

Obediently I did as I was told and then took my place at the table, a piece of rough plywood propped precariously on four blocks of wood. An embroidered cloth covered most of it and plates and cutlery had been set around its perimeter.

In the centre of the table was a tall stack of hotcakes, golden brown and tender, each one the full size of the big frying pans. Beside them stood the tin box of butter, not to be smeared on, melting and disappearing into the vastness of the enormous cakes, but to be placed on the rim of the plate in a cool yellow lump to be picked up, bit by bit, on the edge of the fork and added to each individual bite, its smooth mellow saltiness providing a dot of contrast to the sweet egginess of the flapjack. And the whole mouthful was washed down with gulps of reconstituted Trumilk, mixed extra rich for the occasion with an additional cup of the powdery milk solids. Sometimes, when we got close to the bottom of the twenty-five-pound tin container, the quality of the fluid got a little thin and blue, but this morning there was a creaminess to it that joyously bespoke a full new drum.

We sat for a long time in uncharacteristic silence, busy with our knives and forks, enjoying the novelty of a picnic breakfast. The Sunday morning pancake ritual had its beginnings many years before.

During his years in Chicago, Dad had spent much of his spare time learning the habits and customs of the country, among them the gustatory practice of the healthful big breakfast, which often included hotcakes and bacon and eggs. Of course, being on the perpetual edge of financial embarrassment meant that this was a luxury that could be indulged only periodically and so it became his Sunday morning treat. A few years later, in the small house in a reindeer camp in the Arctic, on the first Sunday after their wedding, my father tenderly woke his new bride.

"Come darling, I have a treat for you." Ceremoniously, he helped her into her wrapper and seated her at the kitchen table, set rather elegantly for two. Turning from stove to table with a flourish, he set a plate before her.

"Madame, your breakfast." Madame looked at the huge flat cake. "What is it?" she asked faintly.

"It's a pancake. We eat these every Sunday. Look," he said, pouring on thick syrup in a gooey flood, "take a little piece, put on a bit of butter and eat it," he concluded with a big smile. He poked it at her mouth.

His bride drew back with a shudder. "No, thank you. All I want is some bread. And coffee."

"Of course, have coffee. But now you live in Canada. And in Canada we have pancakes on Sunday."

"I can't eat it." Flatly.

"Of course you can." Impatiently. "Just try it."

My mother stood up. My father stood up. And for several moments the exchange went on, getting louder and more emphatic. Suddenly, it came to an abrupt end as the bride snatched her coat from a peg on the wall and pulled it over her robe. Dad stopped in mid-sentence and stared open-mouthed as the sweet little woman who had so recently promised to love and, more to the point, obey him, strode past him and flung open the door.

"What are you doing? Where are you going?"

She looked at him with cold blue eyes. "I will not be told what to eat. I will not eat your pancakes. And I am going back to Denmark!" And with that, she stepped over the threshold (the same one he had laughingly carried her over less than a week before) and began a quick march away from the cabin, past the reindeer pens where two Lapp herders watched out of the corners of their eyes, in a straight path out of camp over the rolling and barren tundra.

Dad stood leaning against the jamb, watching her go, smiling a little. After a moment, he went inside, closed the door and sat down to leisurely finish his breakfast. He was working on his second cup of coffee when the door opened behind him and slammed shut with a resounding crash. He turned in his chair to face his angry wife.

"You would just have let me go," she began, accusingly.

"Oh, I didn't think you'd go far." He looked down at her fluffy little slippers, wet now and soiled with tundra bog. "Look here, I've kept your breakfast warm." He took her plate from the back of the stove. "Come now," he coaxed, "just try one bite."

For a long moment, my mother regarded her tall new husband with his boyish grin and thick auburn curls. Gradually, her brow cleared and a hint of a smile began to thaw the icy blue eyes.

"Would you really have let me go?" she demanded.

"No. Would you really have gone?"

"Over a pancake? No, I suppose not." She sighed and looked at her plate. "Only on Sundays? Well, I guess I could learn."

⋅౿⊛ೃ⋅

Now she finished her second cake, tipped her stool back against the black wall of the hut behind her and tilted her face to the sun. "That was good, Bob," she said. "Now I'm too full to do anything, I'll have to go back to bed." She winked at us with both eyes. We smiled back, full of pancakes, full of eagerness to get on with our day.

"*Tak for mad*, Daddy," we chorused.

Dad speared the last flapjack onto his plate. We groaned inwardly at the delay, knowing we would not be excused until he was finished. He reached for the butter dish with his knife, hesitated, looked at us.

"I guess I'm full too," he said at last. "*Velbekommen.*"

We sprang up, clattering our dishes together into a pile and gathering the cutlery, impatient to be done with our chores and onto some serious exploring.

"Just leave the dishes," Mom laughed, "there's no hot water yet anyway and they can wait. Just make your beds before you go. And put on your stockings, Ellen."

Minutes later, we burst from the sleeping hut and lit out running—three intrepid explorers, adventure bound.

Our first stop was at the twelve-hole latrine in the centre of camp. The largest of three such buildings located at strategic points around the settlement, it was of stout frame construction covered with tarpaper. Its narrow plywood door was fitted with a tight spring but remained latchless, privacy not being an army watchword. Inside, a high framework divided the room with six seats facing the door and six at the back, facing the rear wall. Several tattered magazines lay on top of the divider, easily accessible from both sides. With a total lack of modesty, Johanne and I seated ourselves companionably side by side while Aksel went around to the back.

"What are those?" asked Johanne, pointing at two tall, yellow-stained porcelain troughs near the door. "I don't know, Jo. Do you, Ax?" I raised my voice even though he sat directly behind us, separated by a mere few inches of boxed frame.

"Of course, dummy. They're urinals."

"Urinals? What are they used for?"

"For peeing in. Men like to stand up and pee."

Well, shoot, I knew that. I'd often watched Aksel pee out in the bush; admired the glittering amber arc that splattered like raindrops as he directed his stream with great accuracy at leaves or rocks. He'd even knocked an ant off a log once and we'd laughed to see it stagger away from the sudden downpour. It was an ability that I admired and had tried myself a time or two, with the predictable results. It didn't seem fair that he should be able to perform this wonderful feat with such ease and pleasure while all I got out of it was a wet stocking. Not fair at all.

But those things by the door, the urinals? If you were inside anyway, why not just pee tidily down the hole in the seat? It just didn't seem quite... nice... somehow, to pee into a trough and leave it for someone else to look at. Of course, there was a little drain but judging by the look, not all of the liquid had run away; some of it had remained to dry into a dirty yellow crust. Urinals. Well, I was sure glad that women didn't have to use them.

"Come on, you guys!" Aksel's voice cut short my musings and obediently we got up from our thrones and followed him outside. My stockings sagged at half-mast and I pulled them up, moving the small rubber buttons farther down and resetting the metal clasp around them. I groaned. Darn. Darn, damn things. Enviously, I glanced at Aksel's overalls. That was something else that wasn't fair. He could wear pants and I couldn't. Just dresses that were always bunchy and wrinkled and stockings that were bagging and falling down. Not fair, by a long shot!

We continued through the camp, scuffling our feet in the dry drifts of leaves that lay everywhere. The soft misty greens of summer had long since turned sere and brown and the lush clumps of fireweed were dead now, standing stiff and naked, rustling in the slight breeze and whispering of the coming winter.

"'Member how pretty these were last summer?" Jo snapped off a woody stem and held it, remembering. "But this is pretty too," she went on, indicating the elongated blossom stems that were split and curled back dryly. "Lookit how they're all curly, like hair curls. I wish I had curls like this."

My thoughts made a giant step backwards to the previous spring when Betty had walked into the kitchen after an unauthorized trip to Laura's Beauty Salon, where she'd had sixteen years' growth of tawny hair whacked off. The remaining tresses had coiled and bounced in soft natural curls around her face and Jo and I had been enchanted, feeling them and curling the soft silky locks around our fingers. But Mom had been aghast. "Oh Bet, your long, lovely hair!" And Dad had been furious, had ranted and raved, not so much that she had cut her hair (indeed, the new hairdo was very becoming) but that she had done so without prior consultation or permission. Remembering the scene, Dad red-faced and roaring with anger, and Betty trembling a bit in the teeth of the storm but with round chin raised and blue eyes defiant, I looked at Jo's long red-gold braids and grinned. "I don't think you'd better think about curls for a while. Daddy's still mad at Betty." We laughed and ran to catch up with Aksel as he waited for us at the top of a small hill overlooking the river road.

Our camp was spread in an orderly fashion over seven acres, bounded on the south by the Alaska Highway as it came off the bridge and swung in a long, looping curve going west and north out of the valley toward Whitehorse. Halfway up the hill a narrow, well-gravelled road cut off to the right and down toward the river, bordering the camp to the north. This road ended with a bump, smack-dab at our old friend of the previous summer, the massive wooden ferry, lying beached on the riverbank about a hundred feet downstream from the bridge. Between 1942 and 1944 she had worn her bright red paint like a badge of office as she plunged back and forth across the wide blue river, proudly carrying men and equipment from one side to the other during bridge construction. Now, her red paint rusty and flaking, she lay abandoned on the sloping clay bank, high and dry except during spring runoff when the river rose to tug gently at her forequarters, urging her to come for one last run.

As we reached Aksel, he lifted his arm and pointed. "There's our ship, men. We'd best be getting on board."

For the next while, we plied the dangerous river on our noble lady, bringing supplies to the settlers the length and breadth of the Teslin valley. Natives harassed us from the high clay banks but we outwitted them, plunging recklessly through rapids and whirlpools, leaving them outdistanced and howling their disappointment. Later, having journeyed our way from the mighty Teslin to the Pacific Ocean, we took a direct hit from a Japanese torpedo and had to abandon ship, escaping with our powder dry and our bravery intact. Sadly, we stood and watched the old girl sink lower in the water until, with one agonized gurgle, she sank below the waves.

"Hoo-hoo! Hoo-hoo, Ellen, Aksel..." It was Mom coming down the river road, buckets in hand and a smile on her face as she caught sight of her gallant crew. "Come," she said, "Ken Pryor's here with the rest of the stuff and Dad wants you all to come and help. Fill these, Aksel," she commanded, handing him the water pails. "We'll need lots of water for cleaning."

Aksel dipped the pails full and we started for home, two men to the bucket and Mom leading us in song.

"The Emperor Napoleon with his ten thousand men..."

Up the hill we marched, singing lustily, and drew to a company halt before Dad and Ken, marking time on the final "...as they went marching on!" We broke ranks, laughing, and clustered around the lanky dark truck driver. "Hi, Ken," we chorused.

"Hi, kids," he greeted us easily. "Your Dad's been telling me you're all settled in, and rarin' to go." He put his hand on Jo's head. "Hello, squirt, how's my best girl?" Jo looked at him soberly. "I'm good. Did you bring Betty?" she demanded.

"No darlin', I didn't." He caught her under the arms and swung her onto the back of his truck. "But I did bring... this!" he finished triumphantly, pulling back the tarpaulin to reveal the dark polished wood and gleaming ivories of our old upright piano.

Smiles broke out all round at the sight of our treasured partner of a thousand singalongs. Music had always been a big part of our lives and we never missed an opportunity to raise our voices in a bit of spontaneous melody either at the piano with Mom or with Dad's guitar, or simply unaccompanied, as in our enthusiastic rendition of Old Boney's marching song. Now, as the heavy instrument was moved, with a little cussing and a lot of difficulty, into the Quonset hut earmarked "café," we all gathered near.

Brum, brum, brum, brum, the strings resounded in descending discords as Mom dusted the keys with her apron. "Bring the bench, Bubi," she ordered.

Dad hurried out to the truck and soon returned, carrying the long, hinged seat. Throwing back the lid, Mom selected a handful of sheet music and seated herself. Her plump fingers roved the keys in a swirl of chords that covered the full range from top to bottom. "Sounds just fine." She smiled at Ken. "You must have taken good care with it." As Jo and I seated ourselves on either side of her on the bench and Aksel and the men crowded close behind, Mom chose a piece of music and opened it to stand on the ledge above the keys. Automatically, her fingers picked up the introduction.

"Bumty-bum, bum, bum, bum…" Dad's bass rumble counted down the intro and with a flourish of his hand, he brought us all into the verse:

"There is a tavern in the town (in the town!)

"And there my true love sits him down…"

From "Tavern," we progressed steadily through "Over There," "Long Trail A-Winding," "Gold Mine in the Sky" and "Whispering," to "'Til We Meet Again," after which Ken took his cue and his departure, leaving us without a baritone. It was time, anyway, to cease the merry-making and get on with the business at hand.

8

"My mama done tol' me..."

"...AND PUT TWO SLICES OF bread with it... Oh Bubi, do you think they will be alright?" Mom turned a worried face to Dad. He smiled back at her reassuringly. "They'll be fine, skat. Come on now or we'll be late for the dance."

We had been at Johnson's Crossing for nearly a month and except for a couple of trips to Teslin for supplies, our parents had been nowhere. Now, they had been invited to an old-time dance in Whitehorse and if Mom could resolve her stewing and fretting they were going stepping. She resumed her instructions.

"Don't let the fire go out and don't keep the stew too far over the heat." The memory of scorched pea soup loomed large. "And remember to wash your hands before serving anything."

"Yes, Mum, we'll remember."

There were kisses, a medley of goodbyes, one final apprehensive look and away they went in a cloud of dust, and we were left to our own devices. All of a sudden it seemed very lonely. We looked at each other and then away.

Jo sniffled as a tear trickled down her cheek. "I want Mum to come back."

Aksel put his arm around her narrow shoulders and pulled her against him. "Don't cry," he said, "they're only going to be gone for a while and when you wake up in the morning, they'll be home."

"You mean Mummy won't be here to tuck me in?" Jo wailed in alarm and tears began to pour in earnest.

"Come on, Jo, don't cry now," Ax began again. "We're gonna have fun all by our lonesomes, and anyhow," he turned to look out the window, "lookit, here comes a customer!"

Correction, here came not one, but three customers, and now it was my turn to be alarmed. One customer I could care for, even with my rudimentary culinary experience, but three? I looked at Aksel but what I saw in his face was not very reassuring. Three customers seemed a crowd to him, too.

The front door opened and two men and a woman came into the snug warmth of the dining room, gazed around for a moment and then seated themselves at one of the wooden tables. We peered at them from behind the small counter set in the partition that divided off the kitchen. The woman, young and pretty, caught sight of us peeking around the frame.

"Hi there," she called cheerfully. "Can we have something to eat?"

Aksel straightened up, squared his shoulders and walked out to the front. "Hello," he said. "Mum and Dad have gone to Whitehorse and we can't make very much but we have some very nice stew, if you would like some of that, with homemade bread," he finished in a rush.

"That would be just fine," said one of the men, "and how about some coffee while we're waiting?"

"Yessir," Aksel returned in his most professional manner. "Coming right up." He hurried back to the kitchen, where Jo and I still peeked. "Come on, Ellen, wash your hands and fix the plates." He put cups and saucers together and carefully poured the fresh brew that Mom had made only minutes before.

I stirred the bubbling brown stew, sniffing the rich smell. It was ready to serve. I took three plates down from the shelf. Let's see now, what else had Mom told me. Oh yes, some beet pickles on the edge. And a dish of butter. And bread. Ruefully, I surveyed my thick jagged slices. "Ax," I hissed, "look at this."

"It's okay," he whispered back, "now put the stew on the plates."

I took the ladle and dipped out the thick slumgullion. "Is this enough?" Aksel shook his head. "More, I think." Jo added her two cents' worth, "Mummy puts lots on the plates." I added another glop. Now it all seemed in danger of sliding off the edge. I took out a little, leaving a telltale high-water mark. I dabbed at it with a dishtowel. "It's alright, Ellen. Now fix the other ones." Carefully, one hand on each side, Ax carried out the plate and put it down in front of the lady.

"It smells wonderful" She smiled at my brother. "Your mother must be a good cook."

Aksel returned her smile. "She is," he said. He stood for a moment, watching as she picked up her fork and began eating.

"Hey, young feller, how 'bout ours?" The jocular tone broke into Aksel's reverie and flushing a little, he hurried into the kitchen where I was still adding and subtracting for the other two orders. One by one he carried them out, poured more coffee and, in due course, delivered canned plums and oatmeal cookies for dessert. With intense concentration, he prepared the bill: 3 stews... $3. He presented it with some diffidence.

"Three bucks, eh?" the older man reached for his wallet. He extracted three one-dollar bills and handed them to Ax. "Cheap at twice the price," he said.

Puzzled by the expression, Aksel took the money gingerly. "Is it too much?" he asked, hesitantly. The young woman laughed. "No, he just means that it was a very nice meal for not very much money. You tell your mother that we enjoyed her stew and the service was good too." They got up to leave. "Seems like you're getting some more company," she said, nodding her head toward the window, through which we could see a British Yukon Navigation truck turning in past the modest Porsild's Roadhouse sign. "You're going to be busy."

Aksel and I sprang up from the couch as the back door opened. "Dad, is that you?" Aksel called. The place was black-dark.

"Yes, we're home. Were you sleeping? Where's the lamp?"

"Over here." My brother fumbled with the matches and soon, soft light from the kerosene lamp illuminated the room.

Mom and Dad looked around and then at one another. Aksel grimaced. "It didn't seem quite this messy before," he muttered, and all of a sudden I found myself wishing that we had made an effort to clean away the debris before we had lain down to await our parents' return. Then, it had seemed important to leave everything as evidence of our industry; now it merely seemed slothful.

Dirty dishes covered all three tables, and chairs remained where they had been pushed back, as if awaiting the imminent return of departed derrières. On the tables, a few pieces of bread turned up dry edges and partly used lumps of butter settled listlessly in the heat from the well-fortified barrel stove. Filled and overflowing ashtrays told of either leisurely post-prandial coffee and conversation or long delays between courses, probably both.

The kitchen was in a similar state of shock.

The big Dutch oven still sat on the back of the stove, the last quarter-inch of stew dried to lumpy cement. Both frying pans bore testimony to recent use and on the counter, part of a slab of bacon and half a loaf of bread lay abandoned on a drift of crumbs. A sluggish river of purple had seeped from an overturned plum tin, winding a tortuous path around a clot of dried egg yolk and stew-encrusted serving spoon, before oozing over the edge of the counter to puddle, drop by gummy drop, on the floor. On the warming shelf above the stove roosted the lid of the coffee pot, the drip of gravy on it only slightly thicker than the contents of the nearly full pot that still sat on the business end of the now-cool range.

No one spoke as Dad took the last clean mug from the cupboard and poured himself a cup of the lukewarm brew, thick and black as fifty-weight Marvelube. With infinite care he spooned in two sugars and a dollop of canned milk. Round and round he stirred, our eyes following the motion. Mesmerized, we watched him tuck the spoon under his thumb, raise the cup to his lips and drink, three mouths pursing half-open as the viscid stuff dropped by a third. As we stared in fascination, he rolled the coffee from side to side, his Adam's apple bobbing as it went down, apparently in chunks. He coughed a bit as one of the chunks hit a snag.

"Pretty..." Aksel's voice came out in a squeak. He tried again. "Pretty strong, hey, Dad?"

"Pretty strong," Dad agreed. He took another small sip. Mom still had said nothing but now she slid an arm around me.

"We were real busy," I said, helplessly. She hugged me to her. "I can see that," she laughed. Then, more seriously, "How in the world did you manage? How many people did you have in? And did you sell all the stew or did you eat it?"

"We sold it." The sleepy voice came from the corner where Jo had been curled up sound asleep under a grey blanket. "And Ellen and Aksel were really busy and I had to keep care of the money and just lookit!" She held out the wooden White Owl cigar container we used as a cash box. In it were twenty-three dollar bills and a handful of coins. "We got lots of money for you."

And, in fact, we had got "lots of money" for them. It was the busiest supper hour in our admittedly brief operation and we were justifiably proud of ourselves and so were our parents. Proud and pleased.

"I just can't believe you sold all that stew!" Mom marvelled for the third time. "I thought there was enough for two days. And how did you think to cook bacon and eggs when it was all gone?" She shook her head a little as she glanced at the serrated edge of the bacon.

"Well, George McNair came in, and another BYN driver and they were hungry and there wasn't enough stew and he said can you cook bacon and eggs and I said I think so and I did. Ax made some more coffee but he couldn't remember how much grounds and then George said put in a little bit more and then it boiled too much..."

Over the years, we kids would "keep care" of things many times and invariably, the moment the folks turned wheels out of the yard, all hell would break loose and there we'd be, up to our inexperienced teakettles in travellers demanding soup (easy) and breaded pork chops (infinitely more difficult and usually served charred side down and pink in the middle). Eventually, we grew adept at caring for the sudden influx, but I never did lose that feeling of impending doom generated by my father's casual, "Think you can handle things for a few days?"

Truth to tell, we'd probably not had more than a dozen or so customers that evening, but at that, it was still several more than Mom had been serving in an entire day since their opening a few weeks before. There simply wasn't that much traffic.

By the fall of 1947, the highway had been under Canadian jurisdiction and designated a public thoroughfare for little more than a year. And a rough old trail it was, too. Dusty. And if it wasn't dusty, it was muddy. And where it wasn't dusty or muddy, the bare bones of the mountains wore through the gravelly top-dressing and broke off in big and little chunks that got in the way of oncoming traffic and broke axles and windshields. Or pierced tires and radiators, or formed themselves into ridges that sprung frames and doors of the most solid vehicles and loosened the teeth of their drivers. In other places, where the road jiggled and heaved over undrained muskeg underlain with permafrost, or gingerly felt its way across steep, clean-washed floodplains, it had a habit of dropping right out from under, in a way that was disconcerting, to say the least.

Many bridges and culverts were of a temporary design and getting more so with every heavy rain or spring runoff. And there were steep grades and switchbacks that were safe for neither man nor his machines but were expected to be mastered by both. In short, it was not a road for the lily-livered. Nor, given the ground rules set down by the Canadian government, was it likely to improve much in the near future.

The Alcan Highway, as it was known in those days, was something of a white elephant, as far as Ottawa was concerned.

Oh, they acknowledged the need for it in those war-feverish days, had supplied men and equipment and expertise when and where needed with a wholehearted zeal and exuberance, heigh-ho, hands-across-the-border for the common good, and all that. Goodness only knew that should Alaska come under further attack by the Japanese, Canada's northwest would be exposed and extremely chilly. As someone so succinctly put it, "You cover my ass, I'll cover yours!" Or words to that effect. But now it was all over but the cheering and the Yanks had gone on their way rejoicing, leaving the Royal Canadian Army with this great whacking trail leading off through the bush to no Canadian destination in particular and with neither the equipment nor the funds to properly maintain it.

Their mandate specified that they maintain the road as a military highway, but at the same time they also had to prepare for the eventuality of civilian traffic. The lure of Alaska was great and, in good conscience, they could not stop Americans from using "their" highway to get there. They could, however, make it very difficult, and they did, imposing restrictions and demanding cash deposits or guarantee of export bonds on vehicles starting up the Alcan. These restraints, coupled with the advertised scarcity of gas stations and roadhouses, kept private travel to a minimum. And in October 1947, though few passed up an opportunity to stop for a bite to eat or merely to reassure themselves that they were not alone in this vast wilderness, business did not exactly boom. But then, my parents had not expected it to.

There was never any doubt in their minds that they would have more than ample time to set up shop with few interruptions. Nevertheless, with early morning frosts and dwindling daylight, they hastened to the task.

My parents were masters of the art of making everything *hygglige*, a Danish word meaning cosy and comfortable, and their efforts on behalf of prospective customers were unrestrained. Coat upon coat of calcimine lightened the dingy interior of the hut my mother had designated as our roadhouse, and several small

dormer windows further helped to brighten things. A partition
was erected to separate the kitchen from the dining-sitting room.
Three rough tables were fashioned of two-by-fours and plywood
and covered with glossy white oilcloth. In the kitchen, a long work
counter was built along the windowed wall facing the highway,
and shelving for equipment and supplies covered the back wall,
at least as far up the side as the curve would allow. In the centre
of this room, smack between counter and shelves, stood the small
cookstove that had last been seen puffing away out back under the
tarp, and a good-sized woodbox, front-opening and covered to
make an additional work table, stood close by the end nearest the
back door. A white enamelled water barrel held forty-five gallons
of cold, clear river water and above it, suspended on a hinged ring
that encircled its cannon mouth, hung the Dipper.

This was the floor plan. And now came the *hygglige*.

In the dining room, bracketed by bookshelves, a comfortable,
rump-sprung sofa stood against the back wall; the faded blues
and greens of its worn upholstery echoed in the narrow rag rugs
that were scattered about strategically, covering the worst places
in the splintered olive-drab flooring. The dark Stratford piano
filled most of the right-hand partition and a comfortable, ancient
armchair fit neatly under the tiny counter on the left. Blue paint
was applied, with considerable joie de vivre and evident affection, to door and window mouldings, counter framing, shelves,
woodbox, stepstool and Jiggs-the-cat's left flank. The latter may
have been accidental but we all agreed that it did contrast beautifully with his soft orange and yellow tiger stripes.

Bright print curtains framed the view of the highway; pots of
begonias and geraniums softened it; and as winter came on, frost
often obliterated it, but all added colour and variety to the interior of Porsild's Place, as we soon came to be known. A stack of
Colliers Weekly, *Liberty* and *Saturday Evening Post*s, most outdated by at least a month or more, augmented a fairly substantial
library full of Doubleday and Book of the Month Club selections.
In addition to these were dozens of botanical pamphlets, a few fine

leather-bound classics and one enormous, tatty, outdated medical encyclopedia, its chapter on midwifery dog-eared, underscored and marked with indelible spots that may have been droplets of sweat. Or tears. Probably both.

A tasteful "September Morn" calendar graced the otherwise bare expanse of the front door, and several photographs and framed prints added interest to the inner walls. And front, centre and enticingly close to hand, was that preserver of northern sanity, that social common denominator of the country north of the sixtieth parallel: the ubiquitous cribbage board.

Cribbage, or crib, is believed to have been invented about 360 years ago, by Sir John Suckling, a poet and knight in the court of Charles I. Though well-known and admired for his staying power ("Out upon it, I have loved / Three whole days together! / And am like to love three more, / If it prove fair weather."), he was a lousy card player, who, it is rumoured, committed suicide after losing his coat of mail in a gaming room on the Continent. Another version insists that the Cavalier poet was dispatched by his disgruntled squire, whom he had beaten three games in a row. "Prithee, good rogue," he is said to have cackled, "smellest thou aught?" To which the wretched subordinate is thought to have replied, "Aroint thee, vile runyon! Take thou this! And this!" And so expired the Constant Lover, leaving us with a few lyric poems and the dying echo of his final hand, "Fi'teen two, fi'teen four, a pair makes six and prithee, good rogue, etc...."

If this is true, we can only assume that the murderous squire put to good use the other admirable skills learned from his late, unlamented lord and taught his ensuing offspring the finer points of cribbage, thereby perpetuating the game. It is a testimony to the excellence of the game that it survived murder, revolution, inquisitions and religious persecutions, several wars, a plague or two, finally crossing an ocean and thousands of miles of untrammelled wilderness, to become the primary pastime of Northerners of all ages and stations.

Two days after our arrival in Johnson's Crossing, H.V. (Harry) George, superintendent of the central area of the Canadian Northwest Highway System, came to welcome us to his bailiwick and wish us well in our operation. His first words were a gruff, "Glad to have you aboard." His next, "Set up the crib board, Robert. I've got time for one game."

In Harry George's somewhat laconic welcome, we heard the echo of the official NWHS attitude: invitation and encouragement of the private sector. But as well, we heard a genuine personal interest and a desire to be of assistance, when and wherever possible. It was a foundation upon which we built an association that lasted through the years. The advantages were immediate.

Brook's Brook, Harry George's home base, was a highway maintenance camp about six miles south of us. Located between two short, steep hills and nestled in the spruce and poplar on the bank of cobalt-blue Teslin Lake, it was divided into two areas: the highway camp on one side and a Canadian National Telegraph repeater station on the other. It was a neat, picturesque little place. A cluster of frame duplexes housed the road crew and in the CNT area were the long, low office building and several single-family dwellings. The two factions shared a water pumphouse on the small creek, the Brook of Brook's Brook, and generously extended the use of this facility to residents in the vicinity, including Johnson's Crossing.

In all, about a dozen families lived in Brook's Brook, quarrelling, sharing, working and playing together, living in each other's pockets but bringing to the small community the individual customs and idiosyncrasies of a variety of heritages. Scottish, Irish, French Canadian, Armenian, English and Tlingit First Nation were all represented. And now—at the far end of town though we were—Scandinavian.

Someone once said that the Alaska Highway is the longest main street in the world. And we could attest to that. When we arrived at Johnson's Crossing, the community at Brook's extended their borders to include us. Not only did Harry George welcome us and express interest in our plans, so did they all. Within a week of our arrival, everyone had been down to greet us and check on the progress of the roadhouse. Many of them were old friends from our earlier stay across the river, but old friends or new, they all came with gifts of food and houseplants, offers of help and invitations to visit. We were the new neighbours. And some of them were our first customers for things like cigarettes and chocolate bars although "dining out," in those days, was a luxury that few could afford even at our "cheap at half the price" prices.

Coffee, however, was always on the house and there were lots of takers. Harry George (although his "coffee" was usually tea) and Curly Stevenson, foreman of the highway crew; the grader operators and CNT linemen; Metro Solodan, the camp mechanic, on his way to effect emergency repairs on a broken-down machine. During the week, they all stopped to take advantage of the bottomless coffee pot and good conversation. Weekends, a drive to Porsild's with the whole family was a casual social visit, much like running next door for coffee and a few hands of crib after supper.

Pleasant as all this to-ing and fro-ing was, it did not help to put much seal oil on the hard tack, as Dad was apt to put it. And a few truck drivers and the odd intrepid American adventurer didn't help a great deal, either. So there we were, with a cosy little roadhouse, complete with genial host, smiling cook whose rounded contours attested to her skill, a handwritten menu featuring such homey specials as Chicken Fricassee and Meatloaf with Buttered Noodles, and no consumers. Mine host and his lady kept their smiles firmly in place but the corners of their mouths were starting to quiver with the strain. Small wonder they were ready for a night out. And so surprised and pleased with our boxful of dollar bills. It was the first real indication that things might be looking up.

In fact, things were not only looking up, they were looking aloft, sideways, around and ahead. Everywhere, actually, but back. Among the customers we kids had served that evening were a number of American businessmen with heavy-duty interest in Johnson's Crossing, or more properly, the Canol road.

9

"Life gets teejus, don't it?"

I AM SURE THAT WHEN DAD made the historic suggestion that they buy the old camp at Johnson's Crossing and turn it into a highway lodge and my mother casually answered, "Sure, Bubi, what the hey!" or words to that effect, she had no idea to what she was agreeing. No doubt she envisioned a comfortable

The view from the top of the hill looks north into the Teslin River Valley. Within a week, the camp on the east side of the river was swarming with men.

little café with potted plants on the windowsill. Certainly, she saw herself peeling a few extra potatoes and taking out extra pork chops to feed the three or four attractive customers who sat smiling over their coffee as she and Bob and the kids entertained at the piano. Oh sure, there would be a bit more baking and there would be some nights when the dishes would not be done before seven o'clock, but nothing she couldn't handle. After all, wasn't it just more of the same?

And for the first few weeks, that is exactly what she had: the cosy roadhouse, a few customers happy to be there eating her homestyle cooking and lots of time for singsongs at the old Stratford. It was indeed just more of the same, with just a hint of a tea party atmosphere to it all, sort of an "I hate to charge you, it was so nice of you to visit" air. Then, when those lovely people had gone and she had cleared away the remains of their meal, she would whip off her apron and go outside to play. Still smiling and whistling snatches of the melodies we had sung, she would pull on those old overalls with the rolled-up legs and head out to the back forty to gather scrap lumber. Using a wonky wheelbarrow, she'd bring a load back to the café and turn it all into kindling on her trusty swede saw, whose bowed back rested comfortably against her round stomach while she pulled the pieces of board up and down on its sharp teeth as the pile of fire starter grew. When she'd finished playing, she'd wash up, change into a freshly starched and ironed housedress and begin preparations for supper. And it was fun at first, and even rewarding, but not exactly your run-of-the-mill beer and skittles.

There was no plumbing, for instance. Water was hauled up from the river and, later, from the pumphouse at Brook's in barrels and transferred to another barrel in the corner of the kitchen. A big enamelled cooking pot provided water for dishes and Saturday-night bathing. Refrigeration was a screened box on a platform just outside and handy to the back door. And the loo, or "facilities," as one lady rather delicately put it, was a small biffy out back. During the winter months, it was Aksel's Saturday chore to take a two-by-four, kept expressly for that purpose, and knock down the high-rising brown stalagmite, thus ensuring the comfort and safety of our clientele.

We had no electricity; candles and kerosene lamps were de rigueur in addition to a couple of white gas lanterns that got to hiss away their costly contents only when there were paying guests around. Washing was accomplished on a ridged glass scrubbing board in a galvanized washtub; ironing, with sad irons, an appropriate name if ever there was one.

It was The Bush, all over again, with one major difference. Now, we had to share these inconveniences and primitive facilities with a travelling public who were, for the most part, unused to guttering lamps and reconstituted powdered milk and a little house out back with an outdated Eaton's catalogue for toilet tissue. Share them and, somehow, make 'em love it and even want to come back for more. It was a challenge alright, but one that my mother rose to with energy and a certain casual savoir faire.

Then one day, about a month after our arrival, the salvage operations began across the river. Things were never the same again.

Within a week, the camp on the east side of the river was swarming with men and their machines, and Porsild's Place was inundated with business. These men were the front-runners, sent to get the camp ready for the rest who would soon be arriving to begin retrieving the millions of dollars worth of pipe and equipment left behind when the Canol Project had been abandoned. And please, could the Porsilds provide room and board for approximately fifteen of them while setting-up operations were going on? *Could* they? My goodness, they would be only too pleased!

As it turned out, the pleasure was relative.

At this point, we still had no quarters for overnight guests and now sleeping space had to be found for a dozen or more bodies. The Quonset hut just behind the roadhouse was cleared of debris in record time, swept and scoured, and enough iron cots and mattresses scrounged to provide each man with a place to lay his head, albeit cheek by jowl, in the cramped one-room building.

The men had come prepared to rough it and each had his own sleeping bag, which was fortunate because the family linen was in short supply and extra blankets and pillows nonexistent. A washstand was set up with a tin basin, a bar of red Lifebuoy Soap and a meagre supply of towels. Water was heated on the barrel stove in the corner and a slop pail completed the furnishings. It was a pretty rudimentary bunkhouse and crowded, but it beat sleeping on the floor in an empty building in the Canol camp and, at fifty cents per man per night, the price was right. The morning congestion at the little outhouse was a bit harder to handle and many of the men sought out the old twelve-hole latrine on the far side of camp rather than hop from foot to foot, awaiting their turn.

Feeding all these men was, at first, a comedy of trial and error. Used to ordering supplies for a family of six plus a few dozen customers a week, Mom now found herself running out of everything with dismaying regularity. Eggs, eaten three or four per order, vanished like magic, as did bacon, potatoes, meat and butter. Eight loaves of bread, baked fresh each day and brought golden brown and steaming to the lunch table, barely made it all the way through next day's breakfast and now, for heaven's sake, the flour was running low, too. Dad made trip after trip to the small general store in Teslin, one day to pick up eggs and bacon, the next to get yeast, sugar and pepper because those weren't things that came easily to mind when one was making a panicked inventory. With the old White getting five miles to the gallon and that gallon costing fifty-five cents, all that running back and forth was cutting into the profits at an alarming rate.

And then, on top of all that, how was my poor mother to know that when she prepared thirty pork chops to feed fifteen men, five of them would take three each and at least one could have eaten four if there had been more? Or that her biggest Dutch oven did not hold enough soup for everyone and one jar of home-made strawberry jam would not make the rounds at breakfast and a whole summer's harvest was in danger of being wiped out before its time. It was soon obvious that her trusty assortment of pots and pans, accumulated over the years to meet the demands of her growing family, was inadequate to the task when even the old pea soup pot wasn't large enough. After a few days of desperate, losing battle, my parents took stock and the next morning, right after the crew left for work, Dad left for Whitehorse in the gas-guzzling old White, his hat in one hand and a long list of supplies in the other.

At this point, financially speaking, the folks were in fairly dire straits. The purchase of the camp had eaten up most of the summer's wages and setting up the café had nibbled away at the remainder. In addition, there were the ongoing expenses of daily living, clothing and school supplies plus Betty's room and board in Whitehorse. With virtually nothing coming in "off the road," there was not a lot of loose change lying around. There was the possibility of income from the sale of several of the extraneous prefabs (several truck drivers had expressed an interest in using them for garages), but those deals were still a far piece down the trail and there was this little matter of several hundred dollars worth of supplies needed the day before yesterday. On the plus side of the ledger, however, was the reality of the crew that was currently eating up the last of the strawberry jam, but paying handsomely for it, and Dad's good credit rating, although it had never been put to such a stringent test. He laid out the facts on Charlie Taylor's desk.

"Charlie, this is what I've got: a big, empty camp, plans for a tourist lodge, a little café overflowing with hungry men and nothing to feed them or enough pots and dishes even if I had. Think you can help?"

Charlie Taylor was a short, energetic man in his mid-thirties. His father, Isaac Taylor, with his partner, William Drury, had established the Taylor and Drury Mercantile in Whitehorse in the early years of the town's development and had been instrumental in the growth of many other small businesses during the years. They operated from a soft heart tempered with shrewd horse sense, extending credit and advice in equal amounts. Ike's sons, Charlie, Vincent and Bill, along with young Bill Drury, had taken over the family business, expanding and diversifying, but holding to the values and traditions that had assisted other northern undertakings. For a moment Charlie said nothing as he mentally toted up the approximate value of Dad's list and balanced it against the facts, as Dad had presented them.

"How long will you have the crew?" he asked.

"About a month, give or take a day or two. But they are projecting the job to take a couple of years at least and there should be plenty of business even after they get established." Dad puffed on his ever-present White Owl and tucked it more firmly into the corner of his mouth. "And highway business is picking up every day." This was a small prevarication but one that was bound to come true sooner or later.

Charlie studied the list again. "I see Elly needs a big pot... tell George to show you the new pressure cookers we just got in." He stood up and held out his hand. "It sounds good, Bob. Get what you need and pay us when you can."

Dad arrived home that night with nearly a ton of provisions. He had several hundred pounds each of potatoes, flour and sugar; two cases of eggs, packed thirty dozen to the wooden crate; cases of butter and jam and tinned milk and coffee; and a vast assortment of steaks and chops and roasts and stewing beef, enough for a small army. Or fifteen men, some of them with appetite enough to down four chops at one sitting.

In addition to the foodstuffs, there were two enormous blue enamel coffee pots, a round cast griddle and a light aluminum kettle, big enough for soup or potatoes. "Perfect," Mom proclaimed, examining each utensil. "I just wish that the kettle was a little heavier. For soups and stew," she explained. "They burn so easily."

Dad looked hurt. "You don't like it?" He grinned like a fool. "Well, maybe this one will be better." Reaching behind a pile of cased goods, he pulled out a heavy carton, opened it and, grunting a bit with the effort, lifted out the pressure cooker. Dad shifted his cigar from one side to the other, puffed, and took it from his mouth. "Well, what do you think?"

Transfixed, we all stood staring at the twelve-quart machine, or whatever, our eyes as round as the dials and gauges on its domed lid. "What is it, Bob?" my mother asked in a faint voice.

"It's a pressure cooker. See here," he indicated the glass and chrome apparatus on the top, "you fill it up, tighten the lid, put'er on the stove and when that little arrow gets to fifteen, you keep'er there for ten minutes and whup! she's done! It's the latest thing in cooking," he finished up triumphantly.

Dad may have been out a hair on how new a pressure cooker was to the art of cooking, but he did know a good thing when he saw it. The Cooker, as it was always referred to, in tones varying from reverence and affection all the way down to fear and loathing, revolutionized food preparation at Porsild's Place.

Pea soup and hearty beef stews were ready in the twinkling of an eye. Out of cooked potatoes? Scrub up a few pounds and they'd be done before the steaks were. Half a dozen chickens to cook for Sunday supper? Brown 'em in the Cooker, add a quart of broth, tighten down the lid and set the table. All that was left to do was lift 'em out, tender and juicy, and thicken up the gravy. And when it was good, it was very, very good. And when it was bad, we all stepped pretty gingerly till Mom quit throwing things and mouthing Danish obscenities under her breath.

The thing was, of course, that the Cooker processed its load under a fair amount of pressure, ten, fifteen, sometimes twenty pounds, depending on the density and/or the age of the contents. The general procedure was to bring the needle up to the required setting and then lift or slide the pot to a spot on the stove just hot enough to keep it there. It was a simple manoeuvre, easily accomplished by anyone strong enough and brave enough to move the heavy cast-aluminum pot as it spit and gasped spasmodically. It was just a matter of timing.

Timing, however, presupposes the leisure to stand about waiting for needles to rise and precludes the necessity of wandering off to hang up a load of laundry or lend a hand to remove an unbolted section of prefabricated wall, or merely to do a little

PR work with the friendly couple headed north to Alaska in a beat-up old jalopy. And timing was the fragile hook upon which the success of both the business and my parents' marriage hung.

"Bob, Bob, come quick!" my mother screamed, running from the back door as if pursued by hounds from hell. Smoke and steam poured from the open door and as Dad warily approached, the acrid odour of burning food assailed his nostrils. Wonderingly, he glanced back at Mom as she stood wavering between fear and rage. "What happened?" he asked.

"How should I know?" she snapped. "I was just finishing the dishes when the Cooker said 'shuuuuuush' and then it was raining down soup and I couldn't see from my eyes!" She felt her hair. "See, soup on me and my clean dishes and everywhere else and burning on the stove."

Dad came over to her. "You aren't hurt, skat? All the steam and hot soup?"

But she wasn't, just scared and mad. "You see here," Dad explained, "when the pressure gets too high it blows out this little rubber plug and it lets off the steam so that the whole pot doesn't blow apart. It's a safety valve." But Mom wasn't so sure about the safety part.

"To me, it isn't safety, it's just foolishness to blow all my good soup all over. Look, not even two cups left!" she said indignantly. And there wasn't. It was all over the low curved ceiling and on the counters and cupboard. "...And a great big puddle of soup on the ground," my brother sang, paraphrasing "Blood on the Saddle," one of our favourite cowboy songs. Mom impaled him with an icy blue dagger. "You think it's funny?"

Aksel's grin faded abruptly. "No," he muttered, looking away.

Mom went on as if he hadn't spoken. "You think it's so funny, smart guy, you get a rag and start cleaning up." She glared at Dad. "The latest thing in cooking, hmmmph!"

We all helped with the cleanup but it was quite a while before Mom could be persuaded to see the humour of the situation. In time, both Dad and the Cooker got back into her good graces, but residence there was iffy, at best. Over the years the two were to spend many hours sharing space in the doghouse.

The salvage company's advance crew stayed nearly six weeks, giving us a tremendous shot in the arm financially and presenting Mom with the opportunity to learn the ropes while there was not too much else to distract her. It was baptism under fire but she learned a lot during those awful first weeks and never again was she daunted by the prospect of a large group arriving unexpectedly. Her formula? Add some water to the soup, throw a few more pounds of spuds in the Cooker and take out six more chops than you think you're going to need.

When the main body of men arrived across the river, our resident business fell off dramatically, but Dad was correct in his assessment of both the peripheral trade and the increase in highway traffic. By spring, the Canadian government had eased some of the restrictions on civilian travel. The dribble of vehicles going north had increased to a trickle and was promising to increase more following the spring breakup.

10

"Each mornin' at the mine..."

THAT FIRST WINTER WAS A TIME of change and adjustment for all of us. The folks were beginning yet another chapter in their lives under even more straitened conditions than usual. "We aren't poor," my mother was always quick to point out, "we just don't have any money." And we didn't. Any cash coming in from the restaurant was soon allocated to Taylor and Drury (Tiddly and Diddly, we called them) or Burn's Meat Market in White-horse, and the quick fifties coming from the sale of prefabs were soon eaten up by the fuel for the White, lease payments on the Crown land our camp occupied and other more general expenditures. Every penny had to be accounted for. And this was an ongoing source of embarrassment for us kids.

Dad had enrolled us in the little one-room school at Brook's Brook, the first Monday after our arrival. The advent of three more students swelled the ranks to about sixteen pupils, adding Aksel to the present two in grade seven, with Jo joining Bud Morris and two girls in the second grade and me establishing residency in the hitherto unoccupied fifth grade. We came with pencils and scribblers well begun in Whitehorse schools and, as the term progressed, we drew additional supplies from Miss Cox's stores.

Alberta M. Cox was a short, dumpy woman with black and grey curly hair, deep dimples, tiny mouth and the heartbreak of psoriasis. She ran a taut ship, as indeed one must when one is the sole tutor of sixteen pupils over eight grades. She was a competent teacher, but a bit given to playing favourites. She took an instant dislike to me, a feeling I reciprocated in spades. Ours was never to be a happy relationship and it was not improved by Dad's insistence on an accounting.

"Here, Ellen, give this to your father." Miss Cox dropped a small folded piece of paper on my desk. "You owe $2.56 for supplies."

At supper I dropped that bit of information into the conversational pool.

"You owe how much? And for what?" Dad's tone was mildly inquisitorial, but I knew my father and could sense what was coming.

I handed him the scrap of paper with the offending figure written on it. "Well, it's for scribblers, remember I told you I had to get more. And for a ruler..."

"How many scribblers? And how much do they cost?" Dad's voice was growing colder. "And how do I know this is for a ruler or erasers or what? You take this piece of paper back to your schoolmarm and tell her I want an itemized bill, not just a number." He resumed his supper.

Horrified at this turn of events, I tried to explain that nobody got any more than just a piece of paper. It was the way it was done at school. Dad silenced me with a look. "An itemized bill." End of discussion.

Red-faced and uneasy, I stood beside Miss Cox's desk the following morning. She ignored me, concentrating on her penmanship. Finally, she raised her head and glanced at me. "Well?"

Hesitantly, I put the slip of paper on her desk. "Uhh, Dad, ummm... Dad says, could he please have another bill." I looked at the floor to avoid her beady eyes.

"Oh, does he? And what's the matter with this one?"

"It's... uh, it's... um, it doesn't say what it's for."

Miss Cox stared at me in chilly silence. After a moment, I returned to my desk to sit in hot embarrassment. Later, she stopped by my seat and put an envelope in my hand. I took it without a word and, as wordlessly, handed it to my father. His eyes crinkled at the corners as he took in the elaborate address on the front and the completely spelled-out list of supplies within. The next morning he counted out the money into my hand. "Thanks, Dad." I pocketed the money and turned to go into the school. But he wasn't finished. "And here, Ellen," he held the itemized bill out to me, "ask your schoolmarm to mark this paid."

It was not always easy being Bob Porsild's daughter.

All things considered, however, those Brook's Brook school days were happy ones. The school society mirrored the structure of the larger highway community and as our family were welcomed as neighbours, so were we received as co-students and playmates, bringing with us reasonable intelligence, vivid imaginations and good arms, invaluable during those winter months in the Great Snowball Wars of 1947–48 and later, in softball contests between the Brook's Brook Beavers and the Teslin Tigers. As well, I think that no matter how Miss Cox felt about us, me in particular, and our recalcitrant father, she must have been overjoyed to have our true and lusty voices for the Christmas concert.

There was not much for entertainment on the highway in those days. There was a dance once a month, with records for music and refreshments donated by each family and booze bought from the nearest liquor outlet with money collected for the purpose. Crib tournaments were organized from time to time, as were picnics and skating parties, depending on the season. And there was a weekly movie, its procurement arranged co-operatively by the NWHS and CNT, and shown more or less on a regular schedule, weather and road conditions permitting its orderly advancement from camp to camp. But the high spot of the year was The Christmas Concert and it was well attended. Parents, of course, were there front and centre, ready with applause and cheers. It also drew anyone working in the area, including roving highway mechanics, CNT line crews, public health nurses or any other government people staying over in the vicinity. With that sort of interest in the affair, it was incumbent upon the teacher to come up with a fairly comprehensive program and the small school population didn't always provide too much in the way of raw talent.

Much of the material for the concert was homegrown and local characters were written into it, as in, "I want to be Peter Gorst's Christmas dolly." Pete, the CNT lineman, nearly fainted with the pleasure and confusion of being singled out. But that winter, Miss Cox produced a three-part operetta entitled *The Kidnapping of Santa Claus*. It was a lavish production featuring an assortment of fairies and gnomes, the Keepers of the Northern Lights, Santa Claus and his cat Socrates. Johanne, with her piquant little face, quick memory and sweet, clear voice, was Socrates to the whiskers in a costume sewn by Marge Stevenson, and made from an old grey blanket. It had a long narrow tail controlled by a wire hooked over her shoulder and Jo twitched it with abandon and sang her way to stardom that night. She gave a performance unequalled in any subsequent concerts.

The other major singing role in the operetta was that of Titania, queen of the fairies. With a sardonic lift to her thin lips, Miss Cox cast me in the role. I was pleased with the responsibility for I dearly loved to sing, but even at that age, the irony of the casting was not lost on me. With my round, freckled face, scarred knees and chubby figure, I was about the least queenly, most un-fairylike girl in the school. But I could sing, and with my long blonde hair brushed free and shining and in my white crepe paper dress trimmed with silver tinsel, I felt like Titania that night. Even Miss Cox forgot herself and smiled at me and I grinned back. That camaraderie was short-lived, however, and when school resumed after the Christmas break, we were back to our mutual disregard.

Christmas was always a major event in our year, too. My parents went to a lot of trouble to make each one perfect and spared themselves no effort. The house—in this case, the roadhouse—was decorated inside and out with spruce boughs, tinsel and crepe paper bells. A tree, picked with the utmost care and

My parents spared themselves no effort at Christmas. A tree, picked with the utmost care and attention, was set up and decorated with candles and Danish flags and kramehuse.

attention, was set up on Christmas Eve morning and decorated with candles and Danish flags and *kramehuse*, small red and gold paper baskets full of nuts and candies. This Christmas, Dad decided he would go one step further with the decorations and after some figuring with paper and pencil, he and Aksel went outside. There was a rage of hammering and sawing and presently, we heard the old White start up and drive out to the highway. As we stood watching from the window, with a great deal of trouble and heroic effort, our men erected over the width of the highway and to the height of about twelve feet, a rather flimsy tripod. Suspended from this structure was a four-by-eight sheet of plywood with the words "Merry Christmas" printed upon it in bright blue letters. It was further enhanced by a border of spruce boughs. We all trooped out to admire it.

"It's to greet those who haven't time to stop," Dad explained.

"It's a friendly thought, Bubi." Mom took his hand as they

stood looking. "Do you think the trucks can go under?"

"Oh sure," Dad said confidently. "We built it good and high."

The first truck through took it out. We can only imagine the conversation in that long-ago transport:

"Jeez, I musta fallen asleep. Where are we anyway, Mike?"

"We're just comin' down the hill at JC. Ya wanta stop for coffee?"

"Naw, we better not if we're gonna make it home in time for Christmas dinner."

"Yeah, I guess you're ri— Jee-sus kee-ryst! What the hell is that across the road? Goddamn, we're gonna hit— Shee-it, what the hell *was* that anyhow?"

"Damned if I know. Looked like a buncha trees and somethin' blue. That crazy Dane must be hard up for business, throwin' up some kinda barricade..."

We really didn't need barricades. Business was going fairly well without, but the winter was a long one and hard on the nerves. Dad had to make regular trips into Whitehorse for supplies and he'd arranged his week so he could go in on Fridays and bring Betty home with him. It was a pretty good solution to a number of small problems. It dealt with Bet's homesickness because, in spite of her delight in her new-found semi-independence and her pleasant home situation with Don and Murial McPhail, she often found herself wishing to be home. And we, Jo and Aksel and I, often wished the same thing although we would have died rather than admit it. And too, having Betty home relieved Mom of some of the workload that she carried.

Betty was a natural in the café. Friendly and chatty, she was a favourite with the local truckers and the lonely men from across the river, exchanging yarns and wisecracks in equal doses with tea and sympathy. She was a good cook too, and often took a turn in the kitchen.

One morning, she had laboured long and lovingly over a brace of cherry pies. Carefully, she brought the first one around the end of the stove and, kneeling down, inserted it into the small oven,

Betty was a natural in the café, a good cook who often took her turn in the kitchen.

positioning it carefully in the back corner to allow room for the second.

While all this creation was going on, I was dressing to go outside and trying, without much luck, to reach my felt boots, drying on a slatted rack above the stove.

"Would you take down my boots for me, Betty? I can't get them."

She ignored me, patting and poking at the remaining pie, admiring her handiwork.

"Please Betty, I'm too short," I whined.

"Can't you see I'm busy? Get them yourself." Another loving touch, one additional curlicue cut into the intricately carved top crust. At last, sighing with satisfaction, she picked up the work of art, carried it to the oven and knelt down, the pie balanced like an offering between her hands. Jiggs-the-cat chose that moment to pass under the pie on his regal way to the sofa in the dining room. I chose that moment to poke at my boot with a broomstick. The stage was set for catastrophe.

As in a dream, I saw the boot topple from the rack, make a lazy turn in mid-air and land, plop, right on the outer edge of the pie. Like a hotcake flipped by an experienced hand, the pie rose slightly, rolled over and landed on the cat, who squalled mightily in surprise and fled from the room, draped in the much-admired top crust and spraying cherries and juice on everything in his path. For ten seconds, Betty and I stared at each other with eyes as round and blue as marbles. Then, as I stood paralyzed, I saw those other eyes narrow into slits and a fine plume of smoke begin to hiss from my sister's flaring nostrils. Long years of tactical manoeuvring came to my aid.

"Maaaa!" I yelled, bolting for the door and through it, out into the snow and forty below in my sock feet, Betty right on my tail. Hearing the commotion, Mom came out of the sleeping hut just in time to prevent my early demise and I escaped with no more than very cold feet and minor scrapes and bruises. But it was weeks before the final traces of cherry pie were completely eradicated. In fact, when my felt boots finally dissolved during spring breakup, one of them went to its grave still wearing a shiny dark patch where the pie filling had dried and hardened into glue. I believe that's what kept that particular boot together for those last soggy days.

Betty and I mended our fences but it was a long time before I was allowed anywhere near the kitchen when she was cooking. At last, however, I was not only admitted, I was accepted for instruction.

"Okay, Ellen, now you read off the ingredients while I measure them out."

Nervously, I took up the tattered old cookbook, aware that the success of the hot-water sponge cake that we were attempting rose or fell with my ability to decipher Mom's spidery European handwriting. "Ummm, separate six eggs, add one cup singer... uhh... sugar to the yolks, beat well and add, one at a time, six tablespoons of hot water..."

"Would those be level spoons? Or heaping?" Betty asked with a twinkle in her eye.

Flustered, I went back over the recipe to see what I'd missed. "I... uhh... I can't find... it doesn't say..." I stuttered.

"It's alright, honey," she went on in a motherly tone of voice, "it was kind of a trick question. Now, what comes next, some flour?"

"Yes," I giggled. "And vanilla. A heaping teaspoon." Together we laughed, sharing a joke for perhaps the first time in our lives, but not the last. It was a good thing for me that she and I were beginning to find a common ground because the warm and close relationship I'd had with my brother was coming, not to a screeching halt exactly, but rather, to a divergence of the ways.

For the first time since leaving the Sixtymile, Dad was home all the time and Aksel was more and more drawn to manly things and away from the games and fantasies we had endlessly played out. As he approached his thirteenth birthday, he was becoming somewhat aloof and withdrawn. Dad's plans for the lodge had become intensely interesting to him. And he was far more thrilled with Dad's intention to build a riverboat, and set him to taking out fishing parties, than he was in my blueprints for the development of a cinnamon mine in the patch of rusty sand in the cutbank at the far end of the bridge.

I could handle his excitement over the proposed guiding business, in fact, could even see a place for me in there: bailer, swamper, fishwrangler, whatever. But for the life of me, I could not understand his indifference to the Pormor Mine.

It was very soon after our arrival in October that Ax and I had literally stumbled into the gully as we explored a new route to the Morris home.

"Jiminy, Ellen, lookit this." Ax pointed at a point halfway up the bank we had just fallen down. "Gosh, is that ever pretty."

I peered along the subulation of his arm and finger. It was pretty, an area about ten feet long and several feet deep, made up of layers of striated sand, ranging in colour from a light golden brown through mahogany and copper to an orangey-red, all encapsulated in the biscuit-tan of the river silt that formed the bank. "Holy, Ax, what is it?"

Aksel gazed up at it for a minute longer and I saw his eyes go slightly out of focus. I felt a shiver of cramp in my stomach as he turned and put his arm about my shoulders. "Don't tell anyone, Ellen, but I think we've found a cinnamon mine," he said with solemn emphasis.

"A *cinnamon* mine?" I gasped. "I didn't think..."

"Shhh... somebody's coming."

"Hey, you guys... hey, I'm up here." Dick Morris stood staring down at us. "What are you doing in there?"

"We found something, Dick," my brother said. "Come down and see."

Dick was unimpressed. "Aw, it's only some old sand. I knew it was there."

Aksel turned to face us both. "Say it isn't sand. Say it's a lost cinnamon mine and we've been exploring in the jungle and found it..."

"And say we have to build a town and bring our trucks over here to haul it out." I warmed to the scenario as my mind began a review of a recent movie, *Drums Along the Amazon*. "And there are headhunters and we have to fight them off." Considering the chilly wind and the dry bushes edging the small canyon that housed our new-found treasure, it was a plot just a smidge out of plumb. But one we could build on.

"Yeah," whispered Ax. Then louder, as the idea began to ferment, "Yeah, and Dick, you and I could be partners and Ellen could be..." With a hopeful heart I looked at my brother as he paused. Please, I thought, not just a nurse. "...a partner too. And we could call it the Porsild-Morris Mine. No, the Pormor Mine, it sounds better." Aksel and I beamed at each other, and even Dick looked a little more interested. "Hey, yeah," he said, "we could haul 'er to the river... and say there were..."

We had put a lot of time into that mine before winter began

sifting down in earnest. We had built a fairly intricate system
of roads, winding up from the arroyo floor over an improbable
loading platform excavated at the far end of the pueblo-like biv-
ouac carved into the soft silt. Logs, hauled from a nearby deadfall
and hurled into the gully, had been piled strategically to allow
the shorter members of our crew access to the mine area. And
a large heap of cinnamon had been stockpiled, close to the edge
of the watercourse leading from the canyon to the ditch. When
winter shut us down, we left reluctantly but with a feeling of a
job well done. "Goodbye," we told our workers as we sent them
on their loincloth-clad way, back to the jungle that steamed and
jibbered around the edges of our imaginations. "We'll see you in
the spring."

Now it was spring and Aksel refused to come with me to
assess the damage wrought by the April runoff.

"Nah," he said, with a certain impatience, "Dad said he was
gonna start on the boat. And I have to be here to help him."
Crestfallen, I turned and started away. "Go get Dick. He'll help
you with it," Ax called after me.

Dick, I thought scornfully. Dick was no good. He hadn't even
been able to think up names for any of the Indians who had come
out of the tangled trees and vines to help us dig the precious spice.
"How about Giorgio? Or Pablo?" he had asked.

"Those aren't jungle names," Aksel had scoffed. "We have
to call them Bolivar. And Mexicaca and Cuidad." Those names
had sounded exactly right and so had the name for the pueblo
village, Popocatl, short for Popocatépetl. Aksel had just finished
a course of studies on South America but I knew that even if he
hadn't, he would still have thought up those exact same names.
Aksel knew how to do everything just right. Dick didn't. And
Dick was lazy, too, hadn't even helped with the logs, complaining that his back hurt.

Muttering, I walked across the bridge and up to the canyon
and dully surveyed the damage. It was considerable. Meltwater
had come down over the edge of the pit in many places, sluicing

down the soft clay sides and wearing away much of the road we had terraced up the side of the gully. The village was gone. And so was the loading platform. Even the bench of logs had been undermined and lay scattered and of little use. Worst of all, the stockpile was gone, vanished into the floodplain, the costly rubiginous grains indistinguishable in the drying alluvial fan. I sat down on the butt end of a log, chin in hand, and pondered the fate of the Pormor Mine.

"Whatchadoin', Ellen?" I jerked around as Johanne walked into the canyon. "Boy, a lot of water came down, didn't it? Your mine is all melted."

"Yeah," I grumbled, "and look at the roads." I picked up a stick and began grading off a buildup of mud that blocked a major switchback. Jo took up a thin piece of bark and started gouging a flat plane ahead of my equipment.

"Here, let me help get that junk out of the way." She made a purring sound, deep in her throat as she geared the bark down into low and started into the ten-in-one elevation. "Say we're the crew come to get the mine ready. And we're women and can run the machinery better than men."

11

"We sang in the sunshine..."

"Need any help with lunch, Mum?"

Mom spared us a brief glance from the platter of cold cuts she was arranging. "No, the guys" [she pronounced it "gice"] "are going to be late and I'm just making them a *kold aftensbord.*" Literally translated, *kold aftensbord* means "cold supper table," but for our family, it meant Sunday supper, and a sumptuous one at that, offering a variety of cold meats and salads, cheeses, fish and eggs. It often began with a hot appetizer, either soup or *krustade*—patty shells filled with a savoury mixture of creamed ham and peas—and it finished with an apple crumb pudding or custard.

Jo and I exchanged looks. *Kold aftensbord* on a Saturday? And for lunch? "How come, Mum?"

Mom's hands never ceased their busyness while she talked: a pinch of salt into the sauce, a quick swipe to tidy up the rim of the potato salad bowl, an artful arrangement of onion rings on a bowl of pickled herring. "They want to get finished down there today and so they won't be home until they're done and they don't know when that will be. They're leaving this afternoon sometime and I wanted to do something special for them."

"They" were a Works and Buildings crew from the Canadian Northwest Highway System who had come in mid-June to begin building a big garage at Brook's. Harry George had stopped by a week before their arrival for a cup of tea and a game of crib.

"...And a pair is eight and one for His Nibs and I'm out!" he concluded gleefully on a rising note, clapping his hands together with a resounding smack. "You smell something, Robert?" Dad, who was a notoriously bad loser *and* a bad winner, had just smiled tightly as he silently counted Harry's hand and checked the result against the pegs on the board. Finally, he'd picked up the cards in his own calloused hands and begun shuffling them with irritated little snaps.

"You going to let me get revenge?"

Harry had glanced at his watch and shaken his head regretfully. "Can't do it. I'm meeting the brigadier at John's River in an hour. We have to decide whether to replace the culvert or go with a bridge there." He stood up, a tall lean man, immaculate in well-tailored whipcords and grey-blue gabardine shirt. "Keep practising, Robert," he had chortled, relishing Dad's annoyance. He walked over to the partition separating the kitchen from the dining room and poked his head around. "Mrs. Porsild, do you think you could put up eight men for the summer?"

Mom never turned a hair. "Certainly, Mr. George," she had said calmly. "When will they be arriving?"

And when they arrived, Pete Jensen, the crusty old Danish foreman, and his crew of carpenters and carpenter's helpers, she fitted them neatly into the bunkhouse, established a few ground rules with regard to evening coffee and snacks, and welcomed them into the family for the duration. Now that duration was coming to an end and Pete and his crew were headed for Swift River, a maintenance camp a hundred miles south, where they would be duplicating their summer's work.

Casually, I picked up half a hard-boiled egg and put the whole thing in my mouth. "We were going over to the Morrises', maybe we should wait and say goodbye," I said indistinctly, speaking through and around the dry yellow yolk.

"Don't talk with your mouth full!" my mother commanded automatically as she strategically placed a few beet pickles to balance the looted egg plate. "And don't eat any more of those—I haven't got time to cook extra." She paused, checking the effect of the ruby beet slices against the white and gold eggs. "Yes, go to the Morrises'. Pete won't be leaving till late in the afternoon."

Relieved of even token responsibility, Jo and I had left the house at a gallop, reining in as we approached the highway to allow Curly Stevenson to pass us at the turnout. He had been over at the lodge site, talking to Dad. As he pulled abreast of us, he rolled down the window. "Going across the river, girls?"

"Yes, Mr. Stevenson, we're going over to play with Dick and Bud."

"Hop in, I'll give you a ride to the top of the hill."

Curly looked in his rear-view mirror as he drove across the bridge with all the time in the world. He shook his head. "I can't believe how much your father has accomplished in one short summer," he marvelled. "That building's rising like a river!"

Jo and I craned our necks, looking back through the rear window at the big structure rising with authority where the edge of the camp began its gentle descent into the valley. The whole lower floor had been enclosed and work had begun on the second storey, the two-by-four studding of the framing and partitions limned skeletal against the blue-green backdrop of pine forest behind. Dad had made good use of the expertise that had boarded with us all summer. He and Pete had pored long and lovingly over plans and blueprints, drinking pots of coffee, both of them puffing away on cigars. They had often bickered over the best way to underprop and buttress and a hundred finer details, but the grouchy little foreman had been quick to volunteer his men to help with the laying of the long Douglas fir timbers that formed the foundation or the raising of the braced crossbeam that would bear most of the weight of the upper building. As a result of all this help, the lodge was indeed, to paraphrase Curly's expression, ten foot high and risin'.

Jo turned to face forward. "Yep," she said, with great equanimity, "that son-of-a-bitch is comin' right along." Curly let out a strangled whoop. A wave of heat engulfed me and I dug an elbow into her ribs.

"Shhh," I hissed, "don't say those words. Remember what Mom said."

"Well, that's what George McNair said, 'that son-of-a…'"

Johanne was a scrawny little kid, all big blue eyes and knobby knees. Overpowered by her older, louder sisters and brother, she stayed close to Mom for a longer time than the rest of us, mouse-quiet and softspoken, rarely volunteering information without being asked. As we so often ignored her, she in turn went her own merry way, her dolls and herself for company. If she chose to be with others, she would hunker down small and inconspicuous, listening and learning, soaking up information like a sponge. That information would then reappear in the most disconcerting ways, like the George McNair observation.

During the early part of the summer, we had provided a home for an American ornithologist, his birdsong-recording wife and their five children ranging in age from two to twelve. The Wings—was there ever a more appropriate name for a family of birdwatchers?—took rather precarious shelter in the big mess hall. I say precarious because it was being torn down around them even as they camped there.

They were an oddly matched couple: he, a darkly handsome man with flashing eyes and black curly hair, and she, a tall, ungainly, dun-coloured woman with glasses and feet too large to fit into anything but men's tennis shoes. Their two oldest children were boys, and Jo and I got along with them just fine until one day their mother, intent on locating the originator of a singularly haunting melody, happened to come on the four of us swimming in the creek in our underwear. Hopping mad, she hauled Jim and John out by the ears and went flapping up to the café to confront Mom with the horrifying information.

Mom took it pretty well in stride, privately suggesting to us later that it might be nice if any future dips would include our well-worn bathing suits. She was slightly more perturbed after a second wrathful encounter with Mrs. Wing a few days later.

"Ellen, Jo, come with me, I want to talk to you."

Mystified, we followed her into the sleeping hut. She sat down on one of the beds, her eyes on a level with ours as we stood before her. Suddenly, she seemed uneasy. Curious, we waited, saying nothing.

Taking a deep breath, my mother spoke. "Do you girls know what 'fuck' means?"

I felt my knees go loose and quivery, a blush rose clean from the soles of my feet to the top of my head. Even my hair seemed hot. *That* word, coming from my mother's mouth, nearly fried me to a crackling.

Mutely, I looked at my toes, unwilling, unable even, to meet my mother's eyes. The silence stretched out, taut and strained.

"What does it mean?" Mom's voice was a little louder but also, it suddenly seemed to me, genuinely puzzled, as if she really didn't know.

"It means..." my voice trailed off. I couldn't say the words. Indeed, I had only the most rudimentary idea myself.

"It means what the Morrises' dogs do when they're making puppies, you know, co-operating. 'Member, we saw them last summer?" Jo paused, her face calm and thoughtful. "Bud told me that people—"

Mom interrupted, her face nearly as red as mine. "Alright, Jo." She stopped, clearly at a loss, then began again. "Girls, there are words that we don't use. Ever. Only street boys use words like that." My poor mother. The only example of evil she could think of seemed to come from some Dickensian novel and now she had to hear it from her sweet little daughters. "Mrs. Wing said that she heard you say it, Johanne. She was very, very angry."

We stood a moment longer.

"Alright, girls, you can go now. But remember, nice young ladies don't use those words. I don't expect to have to tell you again."

Released, Jo and I quickly exited the hut. I looked at her with grudging admiration. "Where did you learn about that?" I asked.

"Oh," she replied airily, "me 'n Buddy talk about it when we're having tea parties. He knows lots of words like that and so do I now. Want to hear some?"

"No, I don't. You know what Mom said and besides, now we probl'y can't play with Jim and John anymore and it's all your fault."

"Heck, they know just as many as I do; more, even."

Whether or not the Wing boys could have added to our stores of obscenities is a matter of speculation. They were forbidden to play with us again and soon after, with summer drawing to a close and the feathered subjects of their scrutiny and auscultation already on the wing and southbound, the Holy Crow family, as we kids had begun to call them, packed up and followed their subjects back to Texas. For a long, shameful time I believed that the Wings had left because of Jo's and my lack of modesty and filthy language and made a great effort to curb even the mildest profane euphemism that occurred to me in moments of stress. And now, here was Jo, unrepentant and without any evident self-consciousness, using words that made poor Curly strangle on his own spit!

When he got his choking under control, Curly glanced down at Jo, sitting demurely between us. "Did George say anything else?" he asked with a little grin.

"Oh sure, he said that Daddy was a hard-working bas—"

"We're here, Mr. Stevenson," I hastily interjected as we crested the hill out of the cutbank. "We'll walk back to the Morrises' from here." I opened the door and, grabbing Jo's skinny arm, I yanked her out before she could say any more. "Thanks a lot."

Curly waved and as he drove on, still chuckling, we crossed the road and began trudging across the clay flat to spend some time with Dick and Bud, maybe even be invited to have lunch.

What is it about "eating over" that makes it so special, such an occasion? On the rare time we were invited to have lunch with the boys, the fare was pretty dull. There's not too much excitement in canned pork and beans or plain cheese and mustard sandwiches, but we would have killed for those infrequent invitations. And the swapping of school lunches was a bit of daily commerce that would later be reflected in my reputation as an indifferent businesswoman.

We had only one lunch kit, a large black metal box with a white enamelled interior and a high domed lid. Mom used to layer our sandwiches in it, Aksel's on the bottom, mine in the middle and Jo's on top. Our sandwiches were not wrapped, merely separated by sheets of waxed paper. And to make matters worse, or better, depending on the point of view, our mother did not make sandwiches in the conventional sense, she made *smorrebrod*, a lunch-type version of *kold aftensbord*.

Built on thin slices of dense whole wheat bread, our lunches were as colourful and varied in texture and flavour as those Sunday spreads: sharp cheese sliced paper-thin and piled high on bread smeared with rendered bacon drippings; a generous layer of roast beef grazed with a suggestion of mustard and topped with pickles and fine onion rings; boiled potato sandwiches, the waxy slices glistening with a gentle touch of mayonnaise and speckled with grains of black pepper; pinkish-grey liver paste decorated with beet pickles; and always, for dessert, a jam sandwich. By the time we got to school, the lunch kit had been passed back and forth a few times and dropped at least once. As a result, our lunches were a rather colourful conglomeration: cheese, potatoes and meat slices intermingled and held together in their new locations with liberal lashings of strawberry jam.

To wash down the *smorrebrod*, Mom always sent along an old whisky bottle full of cocoa or sweetened, milky tea. At eleven-thirty in the morning, one of us would beg to be excused for five seconds to pour the beverage into an old tin pot and place it on the space heater to warm in time for dinner. By eleven-fifty, the stuffy air of the classroom would be permeated by the rich smell of chocolate, and stomachs would be rumbling in response.

As soon as the Brook's kids left to go home to their own lunches, out came the black box and the trading would begin. Dick and Bud had individual lunch boxes, square tin containers decorated with comic book characters. And, in contrast to our multicoloured salmagundi, the Morris boys' noon meal was a still-life study in sterility: spongy slices of white baker's bread blanketing thin shavings of dry chicken, seasoned with a meagre sprinkle of salt and pepper; the truly dreadful cheese and mustard combinations; tuna paste, a spread that tasted like the second part of its name, only fishier; and for "afters," cookies or, sometimes, canned fruit. By anyone's standards, Irene Morris' lunches were adequate, filling and nutritionally correct, if a tad boring. To us, they were heavenly, and we would trade anything, sometimes everything, for one of those soft white sandwiches with the dry, insipid fillings. Chicken! Without a balm of gravy to moisten it? It had to be better. Why, you could even taste the individual flakes of pepper. And tuna paste, so neat and thin it didn't even overflow when you bit into it, nothing to lick the side of your mouth or wipe off your chin. "Oh boy, Dick, I'll give you my potato sammich and my cheese for your tuna. And the jam, too? Okay, gee Dickie, thanks a lot!"

Dick and Bud lived pretty high on the hog back in those days. The funny thing was, we were the ones who thought we were getting the bargain.

But today, there would be no manna: no one was home at the Morrises'. Cupping our hands against each window in turn, we peered in at the tidy rooms to our hearts' content. Irene was a fastidious housekeeper and seldom were we permitted beyond the big porch-cum-office, which Jack and the boys shared with Punch and Judy and their latest litter of red, white and grey puppies. Most of the available space was filled with Jack's untidy desk, which was full of tattered files and dog-eared reports, and the boys' toy boxes, crammed to the brim with every toy imaginable. We had been in there often, but only a couple of times in the kitchen with its glossy floor and pristine white curtains, and never in the living room.

"Humph, it's not so great," Jo observed. "Hardly any books and no pillows or nuthin' on the couch."

The bedrooms were equally dull, if excruciatingly spic and span. We soon tired of peeping at such perfection and returned to our own side of the river, stopping only for one brief game of hopscotch. Half an hour after catching a ride with Curly, we were once again turning in at our driveway. We waved at Mom through the window and continued over to the lodge site to cheer on our father.

The whole camp had taken on a moth-eaten look. The mess hall had been largely demolished, its lumber transferred to the building area. Most of the prefabs had been taken down and hauled away, leaving only the squared log footings and some of the cross-braces to mark their existence. All of the storage sheds were gone, as if they'd never been. And of the latrines, only the twelve-holer remained, its proximity to the lodge site ensuring its existence, at least for the time being. Heaps and piles of salvaged material lay everywhere: lumber, fixtures, even jagged slabs of concrete saved when one of the pumphouses was torn down. "I don't know," Dad had replied jocularly when questioned about their probable destination, "maybe I'll build a rock garden around them." But nothing was discarded, Dad being a firm advocate of that northern philosophy: never huck out a thing, you might never use 'er but you always got 'er. And, despite the good progress made on the lodge itself, the site still had that raw appearance that made the casual passerby question whether it was coming or going.

Aksel's fishing business was taking off and I was disconsolate that he seemed to be growing up without me.

Jo and I had become good friends that summer. Aksel's fishing business had been a roaring success and as he spent more time with the tourists, who had suddenly begun to respond in droves to the lure of the last great frontier, he had less and less time for me. We still swam and played catch, and he even came to the cinnamon mine once in a while, but his heart wasn't in it; he almost seemed embarrassed. At first, I had been hurt and resentful that Ax seemed to be growing up without me. How could we plan a future when he didn't even want to help me plan an attack against the headhunters who threatened our mine? Disconsolate, I turned to Jo, and found there an imagination and spirit so kindred that if my youthful mind had been capable of such philosophical introspection, I would have pondered and lamented the long years wasted ("long years," in this instance, being relative).

We had begun the summer with a sense of togetherness when Aksel had first sent me to reconnoitre the Pormor by myself and Jo had happened along. Even before that, we had made mud pies together and raised families of Eaton's dolls, but my attention to this had been short-lived and Jo was always being left to bake the pies and tend my orphans. Pies and dolls were all right but wounded airmen and rustled cattle were far more stimulating. Now I was turning to her for companionship and inspiration, and even discovered she had a talent we had never realized she had.

Dad had put the two of us to straightening and sorting nails. After setting us up with a log to sit upon, he stood another on end in front of me and handed me a hammer. "Now," he said, putting an empty washtub beside Jo, "I'm going to bring you some nails, and Jo, you put the straight ones in the tub and hand the bent ones to Ellen. Ellen, you straighten the crooked ones like this." He showed me how, with a couple of judicious, well-placed taps, to turn a useless curved nail into one that could be pounded straight and true into a length of fir studding. He strode away as we squirmed on the uncompromising log, trying to look business-like and ready to do battle, and returned, moments later, lugging a galvanized tub filled to the brim with rusty nails. "There," he said, putting it down before us. "That should keep you busy for a while." He beamed down, stub of cigar tucked into the corner of his mouth, blue eyes squinched against the sun, full of pride in his family who always wanted to do their share.

"Holy cow!" I groaned as he finally left. "We're gonna be here all summer!" Dismally, I took up a nail and sighted along it. I shook my head. "Even the straight ones are crooked."

"Aw, come on, Ellen, it won't be so bad." Jo picked up a few spikes and tossed them into the empty tub. "We can tell stories. It will help to pass the time."

She launched into one of her hair-raising tales of Bloody Bones and his ten frying pans that dragged and clattered behind him as he slunk through the darkness, bent on his nefarious deeds. She was good at it, blending in every fear that preys on a child's mind when the lights go out and the velvet darkness falls thick and suffocating, and adding a few humorous twists of her own. "...And as Bloody Bones' arm fell off, it landed in one of the frying pans and soon it was boiled into soup with carrots and onions by his own mother."

I laughed. "Jo, you always tell the same story; poor old Bloody Bones, he always ends up in something." *Whap, whap.* "Too bad he and his frying pans couldn't come and help us with these darn nails." I straightened a few more. "Want to sing?"

"Sure," she said. "What?"

"We come on the sloop John B., my grandfather and me," I began. Jo joined in. Startled, I stopped singing to look at her. "When did you learn to harmonize?"

She shrugged. "I dunno, it just sounded like I should sing that line like that." We resumed our song, Jo's harmonic transpositions clear and true.

I was flabbergasted. My earliest memories involved a lot of music, either singing at the piano or as cadence for the forced march Mom used to take us on, to improve our leg muscles and get us out of Dad's hair at the same time. As we tromped along, she would make us exquisite bits of lace by shredding alder leaves into intricate patterns, while we all sang of "the Emperor Napoleon" or a "spreading chestnut tree." As lyrics went, they weren't much, pretty repetitive with a word dropped at the end of each stanza and a nod substituted. The final verse was a series of bobbing heads, which ended in a great burst of melody as we nodded into the last chorus, on cue and all still perfectly in tune. All, that is, except Johanne, who always lost a nod or two along the way and came in lustily, two beats behind on the "Glory, glory hallelujah."

When our lungs and muscles had been expanded to a degree deemed sufficient, we would return home and fill our evenings with the wonders of the "Big Rock Candy Mountain... where the lemonade springs and the blue bird sings..." and learned about the Bible with the assistance of a song with the questionable title "Darkies' Sunday School." Those songs, and others like them, had transported us from the bush life on the Sixtymile and the loneliness of an empty camp on the newborn Alaska Highway to a world of fantasy and entertainment where, in our minds, we tasted life in chocolate chunks and sweet–tart drinks. I had loved those songs and had loved singing them with my family, but though we all sang in the octave in which we felt most comfortable, I couldn't ever remember anyone deliberately picking out a harmony.

Leaving the John B. stranded in Nassau, I changed gears to an old favourite. "Try this one, Jo," I suggested, and began, "There's a gold mine in the sky..." Jo tucked her chin down a bit, her soft contralto wavering a bit as she searched for the symphonious melody. She looked at me uncertainly at first, but as the tones blended into a consistently tuneful sound, her voice strengthened until we swept into the final soaring notes with smiles on our faces and the thrill of accomplishment in our hearts.

Music was always a part of our lives, and we were never silent when we were together.

From that time on, we were never silent when we were together. Although music had always played a large role in our lives, it had always been in a family sort of way, Mom at the piano or Dad with his guitar and all of us singing in a group. Now, Jo and I sang as a duet, practising and exercising our new-found tonal togetherness no matter where we were or what we were doing. One would nudge the other and say, "Let's sing." And dishes would be washed and dried in a rhythm that cut drying time to a minimum and ensured a neat and orderly kitchen as we reluctantly finished and moved to rejoin the family at their evening occupations.

Our infrequent trips to town with Dad began a singing marathon that didn't stop until Dad had had enough and would say with a polite, but pointed, "That's enough, thanks." We'd grin at each other and lapse into silence for the remainder of the trip. It was okay. We'd been singing for sixty miles and were running out of ideas anyway. He did love to hear us, though, and often would bumble along in his purring bass or request a favourite, like "Mountain Laurel" or "Side by Side." Even Aksel enjoyed listening to us but his appreciation was more practical, even mercenary.

"Hey, you guys," he would say, lapsing into his still-familiar, high-rolling schemes for our future, "say you get to be really good singers... [What did he mean, *get* to be?] and I could be your manager and we could make records and lots of money..." All of that in addition to the Doberman caper, I suppose, and expanded to include our younger sister. Still smarting from his rejection of our mining ventures and his single-minded attention to his fishing-guide business, I coldly turned him down and forcefully suggested that Johanne do likewise. Famous singers did not need agents who stank of fish and outboard exhaust, especially when that agent got to spend his whole summer on the river while his poor sisters slaved away over endless tubs of bent nails.

Turning my back on my erstwhile partner, I selected a big spike with a definite wow in it. "Jo," I said, as I began tapping, "say we're famous singers," *tap, tap,* "and this rich guy hears us singing on the radio..."

Rejected, but unrepentant, Ax went back to his fishing while Jo and I spent the remainder of the summer hunched over the tubs, planning our future in showbiz even as we recycled the nails to achieve the present.

12

"...and, my goodness how she'd grown!"

GROWING UP AS WE DID IN the relative isolation of Johnson's Crossing, away from the usual giggly-girly relationships with our peers, Jo and I were fairly naive about the rites of puberty. Dick and Bud had proven useful sources of information up to a point, but could never get along long enough for our discussions to ever yield anything truly new or interesting. One warm day, when we were eating our lunch in a willow thicket behind the school, Dick generously offered to let us look at his penis if we would both give him our cold potato sandwiches *and* the Rickety Uncle oatmeal bars that Mom had tucked in for a surprise.

"Haw!" Bud had guffawed. "Haw! There ain't enough there to show for even a potato, ne'mind a whole sammich, haw, haw!"

Dick had coloured violently and, grabbing up a rock, tried to dispatch his brother. We watched as the two grappled and rolled in the dust.

"Too bad," said Jo, absently taking a bite of the desirable bread and potato. "I would've liked to've seen it."

Of course, we weren't totally ignorant. Hours and hours of poring over the coloured plates in the old medical encyclopedia had made Dick's big-hearted proposal redundant, as had our own father's lack of modesty. We had often observed Dad in the raw, as it were, either in the warm glow of the kerosene lamp as he stoked the fire in the middle of the night, or in the bath, stub of cigar clenched in his teeth while Mom sluiced him down with dipperfuls of cold water. We all got that ice-water treatment following a bath. "So you won't catch cold," our mother would say as we shivered and shook and tried to rub warmth back into our goosepimply flesh.

My favourite memory of my father in all his blazing glory, however, is one from the Burwash days, that summer spent building the big log building for the Jacquot brothers.

The tiny cottage that had been provided for Dad would have been more than adequate had he arrived with his battered leather duffel bag, the green frog ashtray and his calendar "girlfiend," Billie. But apart from his normal luggage he brought his wife, four children of varying sizes and deportmental codes, plus all the accoutrements deemed necessary for a four-month stay for six. Undaunted, Dad swapped the single bed in the small bedroom for a double, gave Mom a choice of sides and hung Billie over the other. We kids were laid out in our sleeping bags, like brown twill mummies, in a big, tan canvas tent on the grass on the lake side of the house.

Every day at about 4 a.m., a raggedy herd of nondescript cows, perhaps fifteen in all, bumped gently by our summer home. Complaining softly in the early morning sunshine, they grazed their way to the milking posts at the corrals on the other side of town. Often, we would awaken to the clangour of their bells as they wandered past our open tent flap, and we'd smile at each other with sleepy pleasure and then drift off again. Our father took no such enjoyment in our day-sprung visitors. To him, a light sleeper at best, they were not merely a melodious little hiatus signalling a whole 'nother two hours of sleep, they were a clamorous and ill-bred interruption of his well-earned and rightful repose, indicating there remained only two more hours till morning. And he would roll and toss and thump his pillow, all the while muttering curses in two languages.

One morning we were awakened by an awful cacophony of bells and shouting, the translucent walls of our tent billowing in the passage of lumbering bodies. We wrestled free of our bedrolls, crawled quickly to the door, popped our heads out of the narrow slit in descending order from oldest to youngest and stared with amazement and delight at the scene before us.

Wild-eyed, with udders bouncing and tails skewed aloft and sideways in alarm, the entire herd was in full flight. Flat out and running high, wide and handsome, they were headed for the sanctuary of the corrals. Behind them, no less wild of eye and with everything he owned gilt in the morning sun and swinging with the rhythm of the range, ran our naked father, wielding a long two-by-four with which he punctuated his full-throated commands to "*Ga fanden I vold*, you sonsabitches! *Fordommelig ko* bastards!"

As the cows blundered out of clouting distance, Dad ground to a halt. Still shouting imprecations, he hurled the long board into the dust of their disorganized departure, then turned and strode back to the cottage, a tall magnificent Viking returning from battle.

Grinning, we withdrew our heads from the tent opening and crawled back into our sleeping bags. Betty chuckled. "Boy oh boy, I'd have run too, if I'd been one of those poor old cows." I smiled but kept my eyes shut, a vision of Dad in all his naked majesty etched vividly upon my lids. "Yeah," said Jo, drowsily, "and it wouldn't have been the board I was ascairt of, either!" She was silent for a moment. "Will you look like that when you're growed, Ax?"

A small, scrawny body appeared in my vision, dwarfed by the ruddy giant standing alongside.

"Sure he will." The reassuring words came from an unexpected quarter. "Don't you worry," Betty went on in a kindly voice, "someday Aksel will be every bit as big and strong as Dad."

But despite our studies of the archaic reference book and knowledgeable though we were of outward physical changes, there was much we didn't know.

I got my first period about eleven o'clock in the morning, during an English class.

"Ellen, would you please continue."

I stood. "August is laughing across the sky," I began, "laughing while paddle, canoe, and I..." A tickling little worm inched down the inside of my thigh. "...Drift, drift..." I shifted positions, trying surreptitiously to rub my legs together to smooth away the irritation. "...Where the hill..."

"Ellen, stand still please, when you are reciting." Miss Cox glared at me with more than her usual displeasure.

"Yes, M'am." I felt my face grow hot. "...Where the hills... uh... the hills..."

"Alright Ellen, you obviously haven't studied. Sit down and try to pay attention."

Miserably I took my seat, where I sat in growing damp discomfort until we were dismissed for lunch.

"Your turn to do the cocoa, Ellen. I did it yesterday."

Still sitting at my desk, I turned to Johanne and said, pleadingly, "Would you do it again, please? I have to go to the bathroom."

"Okay," she said agreeably, "but I get to have your jam sammich." She busied herself with the old battered pot and the bottle of chocolate.

I got up gingerly and walked carefully into the bathroom, where a quick look confirmed my worst suspicions. In a panic, I sat on the toilet seat and removed the old pair of Aksel's shorts I had put on that morning, stained now with the dark blood of nascent womanhood.

"Oh damn," I groaned, almost crying. "I don't want this." I crumpled up the shorts, stained part inside, and looked around for a place to hide them. Not the garbage can. Someone emptying it might look inside and find them and know what had happened. I would just *die* if anyone connected me with a pair of bloody underwear! I balled them up more firmly and tucked them in behind the water heater in the corner. Then I cleaned myself with a wad of wet paper towels, bunched a great bundle of them between my thighs and somehow got through the rest of the day. Later that evening, the dishes were done and Mom and I were alone in the kitchen.

"You better tell me about Kotex," I mumbled, glancing away. Mom looked at me searchingly. "Did you start a period today?" I nodded. "Why didn't you tell me when you came home from school?" she asked gently. Embarrassed, I stared at the floor. "I dunno." But I did know. To me, there was something so intensely private about what was happening to me that I didn't want to reveal it to anyone, not Aksel or Jo or even my mother. Except for the necessity of having to know how to deal with it, I wanted it to be my secret. Mine, that is, and the person who found the stained Stanfield's behind the water heater. It was a long time ago, but I still have to wonder what went through his mind as he beheld a pair of men's shorts discoloured by what was obviously menstrual blood.

Jo dealt with impending maturity in a more open and deliberate fashion.

"What is this, Ellen? Why am I growing hair on my thing?"

I spoke benevolently, the weight of almost three years of experience adding resonance and timbre to my reply. "Because."

"Because *why* because?" she demanded.

"Because you're getting bigger and pretty soon you'll start having periods too, just like I do."

"Well, I'm not gonna. I don't like this hair and I don't want to have *that*, either." She slammed out of the room.

Ten minutes later, she was back. "There," she said. "That's that!"

"That's what?" I asked, looking up from my book.

"That's this!" she cried triumphantly, throwing open her robe to reveal her naked body. "I shaved it all off!"

Of course, neither of us was able, actively or passively, to keep the wolves of adolescence at bay and in time we came to accept and even revel in our femininity. Lord knows, there were enough men around to practise on: it was a good time to be a nubile young gal on the Alaska Highway! My father aged rapidly during those years.

The highway was a young man's road. Each spring brought the crews, for putting up and tearing down; for highway repairs and bridge building; for building homes and businesses; for stringing telephone line and surveying and mapping. And for entertaining and diverting the few females who inhabited the small communities along the old trail.

Giggling and snickering, Aksel, Jo and I watched Betty pick and choose from among the many eligible men on the Canol salvage operation. The guys would leave off their pipe-equipment gathering and, under any pretext, slip across the bridge. "Say, Mrs. Porsild, Cookie was wondering if he could borrow a cup of baking powder... oh, hi there, Betty, when did you get home? Hey, there's a movie at Brook's tonight, would you care to...?"

Naturally she cared to. Unless, of course, she had already promised Doug. Or Lorne. And yes, she would just love to come and see the great thundering pile of four-inch Canol pipe that had come in on the last Cat train, and oh, by the way, had Mike Johnson come in with that last batch of pipe? But if the crew from Canada Surveys and Mapping were staying in our bunkhouse, chances are that she might have been too busy to stop and chat, especially if Lyle Westegaard or Johnnie Anderson were in residence.

In fact, there was such a menu of choice masculinity that we were astounded when Betty narrowed her sights down to one, a fireman from Whitehorse. Bill was a rather handsome devil, we all agreed, tall and blond, with a romantic scar on his chin "...where my first wife hit me," he told us, deadpan.

"Your first wife? Did she really?" we gasped in unison.

"With a cleaver," he assured us solemnly.

We accepted Bill into the family without further question. If he was good enough for our big sis, he was good enough for us, cleaver-wielding first wives notwithstanding. Besides, all this cuddling in the corners and kissing on the sly was worth the whole chapter of "Guideposts to Growing Up" in the old encyclopedia. And then some.

"He kisses nice and tidy," I observed one day after a few minutes of peering through the curtains in clinical research.

Bill proved to be a delightful addition to our family, a handsome devil who was full of jokes and pranks.

"Yeah," Jo sighed. "Just like a movie star. And no spit," she added. I looked at her with interest. "Why should there be spit?" asked.

"Well, Bud and I tried some kissing one day, like they do in the show, but it wasn't much good so Bud stuck out his tongue and licked my lips and got me all gunky. He said that was how it was s'posta be but I didn't like it so I just hit him." She grinned. "I'll bet he won't try that again."

Bill proved to be a delightful addition to the group, full of jokes and pranks. Not too long after he and Betty had stood under the white and silver wedding bells in the lobby of the lodge and sworn love and obedience till death did them part, he enlisted our aid in a roguish bit of mischief that has been recorded in the Porsild Chronicles very close to the top of the list.

The highway, in the early '50s, had not improved very much. Despite the best efforts of the Canadian Northwest Highway

System, it was still a ragged, cross-grained thoroughfare. But the traffic continued to flow, heavier and heavier every year, and the increased movement over the road exacerbated its worst problem: dust. The material used to top-dress the surface of the road was a mixture of crushed gravel and clay. When it rained, this compound was bad enough—a slimy, slippery ooze with a mind to take you sideways and backwards and nearly anywhere except where you wanted to go. But when it was dry it was much worse.

After a long spell with no rain, the wonder was that there was any surfacing left on the road. It all seemed to be on the trees that lined the highway or on the faces or in the lungs of the poor souls who drove it. Indeed, it permeated the atmosphere, flavouring the air we breathed and distempering our prismatic sunsets. The dust hung like a dense fog over the road, obscuring the right-of-way and any vehicles approaching in your lane. On a windless day, the suspended particles of dirt would roll like rain down the windshield of a following car and wipers would have to be used to clear a line of vision. For variety, intermingled in the fine dust and dirt were larger fragments of rock, each one a potential broken headlight or pitted windshield. Alaska Highway Stars, these pits were called, and no conveyance was exempt. The trick was to see how many hits could be sustained before vision became so distorted as to be a hazard. The record was in the hundreds.

Broken headlights, however, were a rather more serious matter. It took only one well-placed stone to take out a light, two to stop progress entirely. The dust was often so thick and impenetrable that it was against the law to drive with the lights off and to do so was inviting a head-on collision. Most travellers carried extra sealed beams, and many methods of protecting the headlights were tried, including metal grids and elaborate mesh boxes. None had proven very effective. Then came a breakthrough—the incorporation of a material that had been around for a while but was only now coming into its own. We got our first view of it one summer morning.

"Aye, Les, c'mere a minute," Bill called through the open kitchen window.

Les Allen was a young Englishman who had shown up on our back stoop with his partner, William Whitmore. They had mined and prospected in various areas of the Yukon and just lately had bought a bit of property on the Teslin, about three miles down-river. Today, Les had come up in their big flat-bottomed riverboat and was having a "mug up," as he called it, before returning. He got up to see what was going on.

"Blimey," he said, running his hand through his thick blond hair. "What've ye got there then, mate?" He went out the door, Ax, Jo and I right behind. We grouped ourselves around Bill on the back step, peering past him to share his discovery. Parked in front of the lodge was a pale blue late-model DeSoto, gift-wrapped fore and aft in cardboard and screening, and, protruding from the front headlights, large clear-plastic cones.

"Crikey, a bloomin' breastworks!" Les breathed.

We snickered at Les' terminology, but the choice of words was apt. The heavy protectors that jutted proudly from either side of the ornate chrome grille did look like mammalian protrusions. "Bazooms," in Aksel's idiom.

In addition to the cones, the DeSoto's owner, obviously acting on the advice of some earlier survivor of the highway, had spared himself no bother to safeguard his "robin's egg blue" beauty against the ravages of the road.

The clean lines of the sedan had been obscured with cardboard, discarded boxes that had been opened out, wrapped around and taped on. "Kellogg's Corn Flakes" one door advertised, while the other touted "Kleenex—It Pops Up!" The heavy corrugated paper also covered almost the entire windshield, with only a foot-square opening on the driver's side for visibility. A small star in one corner of the square showed that even such extreme measures had not proven totally successful. Much of the proud chrome grille had been covered with sticky black electrical tape and a wide rubber apron was stretched beneath the vehicle from stem to stern to protect the vulnerable underbelly from spurting rocks. From the grille over the top to the back fender, a wire-mesh extension of the resilient rubber buffer had been secured with lacings of haywire.

All this loving labour had been largely for naught, however, as wind and weather road conditions had combined to sabotage the protective shield. Great holes gaped in the mesh and the leading edges of the cardboard were torn and feathered back in fringes, so that the whole effect was one of a mobile haystack.

As we watched, a thin, anxious man emerged from the interior of the tatty automobile. Ignoring our apparent interest, he took a cloth from his pocket and began a minute inspection of his blue treasure. Tutting and clucking with dismay, he patted and polished, pulled and tugged the various coverings, now exposing, now concealing. At the front, he knelt to give extra attention to the plastic cones, his fingers lingering in a loving way on the dents and scratches. Finally, inspection over, he rose and started for the lodge entrance. Halfway there, he stopped, and cast a suspicious glance in our direction. Then he retraced his steps, returning to his car and ostentatiously locking the door. Satisfied with this final safeguard, he walked quickly through the front door and into the lodge.

Back in the kitchen, Bill turned to us, bushy eyebrows knit intently over mirthful eyes. He looked past us to Betty, who stood by the sink putting a Sunday shine on a trayful of glasses.

"Betty." He pronounced it as two words. "Bet-tee, have you got an old brassiere...?"

"No!" Betty spoke sharply before he could finish.

Les picked up on Bill's idea. "Ah, come on, luv," he wheedled, "an auld one that ye'd not be wantin' again."

"No," Betty said again. "I know what you're up to and—" But now Bill had his arm around her and was hauling her off to the side for a little friendly persuasion while we all watched from the corners of our eyes. At first she held firm, shaking her head and tightening her lips. I thought about the last time we had "borrowed" her bra. "She'll never let them have it," I whispered to Aksel.

"Sure she will, Bill can talk her into anything," he said confidently. "Look at that!" Even as Ax spoke, Bill gave Betty a hug and released her. Flustered and a bit rosy, she left the room, but moments later she was back, handing Bill the sturdy though well-worn lace and satin undergarment.

"Perfect!" pronounced Bill, shaking open the cups and holding it up for Les' approval.

"Roight, cut 'er 'ere and 'ere," the Englishman paused, considering. "Use a bit o' string crost 'ere and 'ook the straps ower the moulding."

Suiting action to words, Bill and Les set about their mischief.

Snipping the bra in two, they took the cups and fitted each one neatly over most of the breastlike protuberance on either side of the car. A long piece of elastic was found and pinned from cup to cup across the grille. Bill glanced over his shoulder. "Ellen, Jo, we need your ribbons."

After slipping them from the ends of our braids, we quickly retied them into bows, which were incorporated into the design.

The two pranksters stepped back to view the effect.

"Whaddye think, mate?" Les asked, his head cocked critically as he inspected their creation.

Bill studied it. "Still needs something. Just a minute." He went into the kitchen and quickly returned. "Here," he said, rubbing a red crayon on the peak of each satin-covered cone. "I think that's got it."

Laughing softly in the summer sunshine, we stood there enjoying the joke. More than ever now, the front of the car resembled a full-bosomed matron. Suddenly Betty rapped on the glass. "He's coming!" she mouthed. Speedily we dispersed, then reconvened at a window to watch the show.

The angular man walked briskly to his car and looking neither right nor left, unlocked the door and folded himself underneath the wheel.

"Oh boy," Ax chortled, "he didn't even notice."

A scant breath later, the "Kellogg's" door opened and the man got out. Taking his trusty cloth from his pocket, he meticulously wiped and polished the small starred aperture in the windshield covering. Then he leaned back into the interior and we saw the lights come on behind the red-tipped satin. Mr. DeSoto came forward to check them, then stopped dead, his face blank with shock.

He stood there unmoving for at least a count of twenty. Then, tense with anger, he yanked first one, then the other offending scrap of fabric from his car, bunched them up and flung them into the dirt. Setting his foot upon the satin, he ground it further into the dusty yard. He glared around, but we held ourselves well back from the window, and finding no one upon whom to vent his rage, he spat once into the dust, got into the car, slammed it into gear and roared out onto the highway, cardboard waving and the slipstream whistling through the wire mesh.

Convulsed with glee, we hoo'd and haw'd and guffawed for a while, then trooped out to retrieve the sorry remains of our little joke. Bill picked up one earth-stained bit of lace and smoothed it gently in his big hands.

"I dunno, guys, I thought it looked pretty fine." He spoke regretfully, brows pulled down in a straight bar over his nose. Then he squinted toward the road where the dust of Mr. DeSoto's departure was just beginning to settle. "You know," he said, fingering the scar on his chin, "that fellow was a little bit like my first wife… she didn't have much of a sense of humour either."

13

"Even though we ain't got money..."

THOUGH MY SISTERS AND BROTHER and I grew and developed in fits and starts, this was not the case with the lodge (at least in the physical sense: the philosophy of running such an operation evolved much more gradually). From a dream and a heap of salvaged lumber, the edifice rose quickly and by the end of our first full year in Johnson's Crossing, the "son-of-a-bitch" that had been "comin' right along" in August had attained full growth. The bare bones, clearly visible on that memorable afternoon when Jo had caused Curly Stevenson to nearly swallow his cud, had been neatly covered over and a shallow hip roof had topped off the structure. Little remained of the old hall, but as it had yielded its lumber, board by board, the new building had achieved shape and form and, on the anniversary of our arrival, we assembled before it.

"Well?" my Dad asked jovially. "What do you think?"

It was a rhetorical question. It mattered not in the slightest what we thought of it or if, indeed, we had any thoughts at all about it. Privately, of course, we had, but a rampaging grizzly could not have persuaded us to utter them out loud. Like the cowards we were, in the face of our sire's exception to our childish honesty, we stood there and lied through our teeth.

"It's good, Dad."

"It's beautiful."

"George McNair says that it sure is a huge son-of—" I jabbed Jo with my elbow before she could complete the quote. "A huge big building," I substituted lamely.

Dad's sandy eyebrows rose, wrinkling the broad expanse of forehead into furrows of consternation. He turned to Mom. "Damning with faint praise, d'you think?" he asked her, a hint of a smile hovering at the corners of his mouth.

Quick to intercede, Mom rushed into the breach. "Ah, Bubi, they are just children. They don't know how to say what they feel. It *is* beautiful and we are all very proud!"

We were all proud, but in fact it was not a beautiful structure. Rising some thirty feet above its rough fir foundations, it resembled a two-storey box, all angles and sharp edges, its many windows like empty eyes reflecting the raw ground upon which it squatted in a curiously temporary manner. A pale epidermis of brand new shiplap had covered a multitude of sins and contrasted nicely with the silvery-black tarpaper laid over the nail holes and splinters in the roof, but did little to disguise the starkly utilitarian overall design. No, beautiful it wasn't, but it was tangible testimony to our father's diligence and unstinting labour. In six months he had almost single-handedly delivered on his cap-in-hand presentation to mercantile magnate Charlie Taylor one year earlier. He had built his tourist lodge.

Of course, the term "tourist lodge" might have been just a tad grandiloquent for our new place of business when we opened in the spring of '49.

In the first place, there were not very many tourists, per se, and in the second, the word "lodge" evokes an image of a substantial log chalet, its burnished amber surface reflecting the cheery blaze in a fieldstone fireplace. Handsomely attired guests lounge gracefully on butter-soft leather furniture and gentle laughter eddies in warm currents. A delicate Mozart theme provides a pleasant musical backdrop to clever and stimulating conversation. As the hour grows late and genteel yawns are smothered behind discreet hands, a gracefully curving staircase beckons those below

Beautiful it wasn't, but Johnson's Crossing Lodge was tangible testimony to our father's unstinting labour.

to the second floor, where snug chambers await. Inside are soft beds piled high with plump cushions and downy comforters. On the floor, thick fur rugs eagerly invite questing bare feet. To further soothe the weary traveller with clouds of scent and billows of rich lather, in the adjoining *salles de bain*, shining faucets gush frothing cascades into gleaming porcelain baths.

Johnson's Crossing Lodge did not have a whole lot of the above: not the burnished logs, nor the fireplace, or even the hot water. Hot water? Heck, we didn't even have running water except when my mother gave one of us a steaming jug and urged its delivery with all possible speed. We delivered much water during those years that I always thought that was what Dad meant when, with a broad wink, he used to advertise "hot and cold running chambermaids." In retrospect, remembering Dad's somewhat bawdy turn of mind, I guess we didn't fit the bill. Nor did much else that the word "lodge" implied.

The amber surfaces? Try flat plywood expanses covered in beige wallpaper patterned with a repeating leafy glade design. A barrel stove with a US Quartermaster Corps logo on the side gave comfort within its immediate vicinity and an eclectic assortment of well-used and unrelated furniture provided seating for our infrequent guests, handsomely attired or otherwise. There was a ninety-degree turn at the bottom of the stairs, but the board risers and unadorned treads led not to sybaritic seraglios, but to a chilly, dimly lit hall from which opened eleven even chillier bedrooms, sparsely fitted in early American army left-behinds. A chemical toilet—the Throne—held place of honour, front and centre in the unisex washroom, and if the wayfarer was hoping for a bath, he was plumb out of luck except for the jug of hot water dispensed on request and delivered on the plod by a lukewarm pre-adolescent domestic after a brief argument ("It's your turn!" "No, it's yours, I did it last!") settled by a decisive maternal clap to the appropriate hindquarters.

Of course, there was laughter, great guffaws of it as our genial host regaled guests and family alike with tales of heroic adventure only slightly exaggerated to improve their entertainment value. And while Mom could tinkle out the most fragile of Mozart's airs, she was happiest playing accompaniment for a lusty singalong. All in all, we were a pretty plain-Jane operation.

As for the weary traveller, he might have been a truck driver. A salesman. A highway worker. He might have been a GI on rotation to Fort Richardson in Alaska, or a whole family of Oklahomans driving a rattle-bang old junker piled high with farm implements, household furnishings and an astonishing assortment of kids and dogs, all on their hopeful way to a homestead in the newly accessible Last Frontier. Almost certainly, in those early days, he was not a tourist. And, just as certainly, he really didn't care that the old sofa and chair in the lobby were not a matched set. Or that the guest register was a lined scribbler, or if the tune that lingered in his mind as he felt his way to bed by the guttering light of a coal-oil lamp was Tchaikovsky's

"Petite Waltz" or the last spirited chorus of "Waltzing Matilda." He was happy to be off the old cow trail, filled with hot food and good fellowship, and his sigh, as he pulled the rough blankets up to his chin, was one of gratitude that he did not have to find uneasy rest on the truck seat. Not tonight, at least.

Those travellers may well have been the least demanding, most easily pleased customers of our career. Highway services were still in the rudimentary stages. In some areas, the Northwest Highway System still grudgingly provided food, gas and lodging of sorts, although it was trying desperately to rid itself of that responsibility. Private enterprise was being encouraged to take over the feeding and bedding of those early pilgrims, and oil companies were invited to set up filling stations along the way. Though development of facilities in larger settlements such as Fort Nelson and Watson Lake was accomplished in relatively short order, the smaller, isolated stopping places were slower to appear and even several years after the Alaska Highway had been designated a public thoroughfare, roadhouses and gas pumps were still few and far between. No wonder those first patrons smiled in anticipation of a sponge bath in a tin basin. Anything was better than nothing! They were happy just to be warm and fed, with a roof over their heads.

And it was a good thing, too, that they were so easily satisfied because as simple and unpretentious as their requirements were, those were precisely what my parents were prepared to offer at the time.

The bedrooms upstairs were spartan. Dad liked to sleep in a cold room and couldn't imagine that anyone would prefer it any other way.

"The rooms are nice and cool for sleeping," he'd explain proudly to overnight guests as he showed them up, "and if you want it warmer, just leave your door open a little." Most guests left their doors wide open to take advantage of the meagre warmth that circulated up the stairwell. This made the last task of my mother's day easier.

The winter wood—part of it! On really cold nights, Elly brought our guests old whisky bottles filled with hot water.

Moving down the hall, she would pause before each door. "Are you comfy?" she'd ask. "Would you like another blanket?" If the reply was an affirmative, she would bring the extra covering and spread it over the recumbent guest, or guests in the case of a matched pair, tucking it in and finishing with a little pat. On really cold nights, she brought around old whisky bottles filled with hot water and wrapped in old towels. "There," she'd say, thrusting her little bundles in at the foot of the bed and pulling the blankets tight again. "Is that better?" I don't know whether she ever kissed their sleepy brows like she did ours following a similar ritual, but given my mother's capacity for nurturing, it's entirely possible that she did.

After ensuring the comfort of her charges, Mom would go to her own icy chamber where Dad waited, smoking his last White Owl of the day, warming her side of the bed like a giant, fuzzy hot-rum decanter. She, like most of our staying customers, would have preferred a more temperate climate. They all settled for what they got.

Later, a furnace in the basement with ducts leading up to the hall and transoms above each door would do much to take the chill off all but the coldest nights, but most doors remained open and Mom continued to make her nightly rounds. It was a custom that made Johnson's Crossing not necessarily a lodge, but a home.

As for the paucity of furnishings upstairs and down, don't forget my parents' skill at making *hygglige*. The old furniture didn't exactly fill the big lobby and the walls were mostly unadorned except for the scantily clad nymphs cavorting in the aforementioned bosky glades. Wide-open spaces of olive drab plywood showed every footprint to lead a prospective customer on the long haul from entrance to dining room. But islands of comfort were created in those empty spaces and the good smell of fresh bread baking and sheer voluble presence of the Porsild family ensured a warm reception that far exceeded the promise on the welcome mat by the front door. And as the year wore on, it all got better.

An auction in Teslin yielded a beautiful beige area rug, which expanded the margins of one island into an area of conviviality and cut down enormously on the olive drab. A nearly new chesterfield suite and a number of end tables were purchased from a family leaving Brook's to move to another camp. Roy Shaw, an RCMP officer stationed in Teslin, filled his long evenings making exquisite parquet coffee tables. Mom bought one for Dad for Christmas. He gave her a brace of railroad jacks, needed for lifting and buttressing the foundation timbers, and we kids received books and were encouraged to add their colourful bindings to those already doing decorative duty in several new ceiling-high bookshelves. With attractive rose-printed drapes bracketing the sparkling multipaned windows, a vast assortment of flowering plants, and crisp white doilies on everything but the barrel stove, we were looking pretty *hygglige*, alright.

Despite all the "cosy and comfortable," however, many things were sadly lacking.

It was decided, early on, that the smaller floor spaces in the bedrooms could be made sufficiently warm and attractive with an abundance of chromatic (and cheap) rag rugs. Downstairs, it was a different tale altogether. The plywood floors were splintery and hard to clean, so linoleum was high on the list of priorities. Indeed, with eighteen hundred square feet to cover, it was a major, major prerequisite. So was electricity. And plumbing. And hand in hand with electricity and plumbing came the appliances necessary for the successful operation of the business. The old wood stove in the kitchen, an old US Army range, was big and efficient, its oven large enough for a dozen loaves of bread. But it had no grill and all frying and grilling had to be done in big cast-iron pans. Toast, too, was made on racks laid on the surface of the stove, but it was not very satisfactory. Either the toast spitefully burned itself black the minute you turned your back, or else it just lay there, drying out, sullenly refusing to tan no matter where the racks were placed. Water was still being heated in an assortment of pots and kettles; refrigeration was an icebox that entailed blocks of ice being laid down in a sawdust pit early in the spring. And washing and ironing of clothing and bed linen was the same endless, back-breaking chore it had always been, only daily now, with everyone helping.

So right up there with lino and plumbing and electricity were a freezer and refrigerator, water heater and proper sinks, toaster and mixer. The hodgepodge assortment of dishes had to be replaced with proper hotel china. More bedding was required, and a washing machine and electric iron to smooth those countless linen acres. The list was as never-ending as the chores and even though business was settling down to a steady trickle, the cash it generated seemed to flow out the back door in the same old volume. It was obvious to everyone that if the business was to grow and thrive, money must be found to deal with those priorities.

Fortunately, there were other men like Charlie Taylor, men of vision and perception, who believed in the future of the Yukon and recognized the importance of the Alaska Highway in the scheme of things. Chief among them was Arthur Pettley-Jones, manager of the newly established Whitehorse branch of the Bank of Montreal.

Dad's first meeting with Pettley-Jones came as a direct result of an unproductive discussion with Thomas Hardie, long-time manager of the Canadian Bank of Commerce. He had gone to Hardie for a loan and on the demand for collateral, had produced a variety of photographs of his pride and joy, his tourist lodge. Hardie had rejected both the request and the collateral out of hand with a curt, "What good to the Bank of Commerce is a half-finished building on a highway that will never be of use to anyone?" Angrily, Dad had stomped out of the bank and, puffing furiously on his cigar, had crossed rutty, dusty Second Avenue to enter the lobby of the Whitehorse Inn where the Bank of Montreal had set up temporary shop. Business in the new bank was not brisk and the young manager in the neat grey suit had jumped to his feet and extended a cordial hand.

"Good afternoon, I'm Arthur Pettley-Jones, at your service." After introducing himself and giving a brief explanation for his presence there, Dad laid the photographs on his desk.

The young man picked up each one, examining every detail with an interested eye. He glanced up at Dad. "And it's going to be a tourist lodge, you say?" He flipped through the photos again. "How may I help you?"

Dad was not in the least bit shy about letting him know exactly how he could help and before long, the two men were up to their teakettles in facts, figures and the rate of compound interest. By the end of the afternoon, the bank had a brand new customer and Dad had a new business associate.

A close friendship grew out of that meeting and the young bank manager was a frequent visitor at the lodge. Nervous as a bride, Dad prepared for his first visit. Everything must be perfect.

"Here, you kids, put these books away. Are these your boots? Get them out of the front room. Aksel, fill up the woodbox. Ellen and Jo, straighten those papers...."

Tote dat barge, lift dat bale, we'd thought resentfully as we hastened to comply with Dad's demands. We watched him pace back and forth the length of the building, shifting the position of a chair on his way through the dining room, re-aligning it on the back swing. An ornament was moved fractionally, a pillow plumped. Suddenly, he stopped pacing and looked around.

"Elly, where are the new magazines?" he demanded.

Mom paused in her lunch preparations and came to the door. "Which magazines?"

"The *Time* and *Newsweek* that came yesterday. Where are they?"

"They're in the magazine rack, of course. Where else should they be?" Mom asked, with some asperity.

"They should be out on the table where Pettley-Jones can see them and know that we are interested in world affairs," Dad snapped as he strode back to locate and strategically advertise his worldly minded sophistication. Mom followed him into the lobby.

"Bubi," she said softly. "Bubi, it's alright, Mr. Pettley-Jones will find everything is as you said. Come now," she cajoled, taking his arm and gently leading him to the kitchen table. "Have coffee. And relax!"

Halfway through the coffee Mom glanced out the window. "I think he's here," she said.

Dad leaped to his feet and hurried into the lobby. Grabbing up one of the news periodicals, he flung himself into his favourite chair and began reading intently. The front door opened. Slowly, Dad lowered the magazine, and peered over the top. "Well, well, well," he exclaimed in mild surprise. Ostentatiously draping *Time* over the arm of his chair, he began to rise. "Elly," he called. "Look who's here!"

Under the auspicious management of Art Pettley-Jones, the Bank of Montreal loaned Dad the money required to finish the lodge. Eventually, the wherewithal was apportioned according to degree of need: desperate, despairing, despondent, or just plain desirous!

Floors were covered with a dark red battleship linoleum, juice was set to flowing from a huge, third- or fourth-hand Hercules diesel generator to electrical outlets, and a commercial wringer-washer churned worn linen to rags and tatters, but clean and white nonetheless. Jo and I proudly carried guests' orders, laid out on glistening white plates with fluted rims, and took coffee around in unchipped cups with matching saucers. Scraping toast became a lost art. And, perhaps most appreciated of all, a flush toilet put an end to the faint miasma that used to waft down from the Throne on a warm day.

It took a while longer for a name for the new lodge to appear out of the smoke and dust of its construction.

Porsild's Place or Porsild's Roadhouse had been the preferred names for the little café in the old Quonset hut, but neither seemed appropriate for a "tourist lodge." Suggestions solicited from customers and neighbours included Teslin River Inn, Sourdough's Roost and Alcan Hotel. Aksel and I both thought Cutbank Inn or Hootalinqua Hotel were prime choices. Jo opted for Cinnamon Lodge; Mom and Betty went with Riverside Inn. And Dad rejected all of the foregoing and chose instead to play up the good fishing in the river.

"Big Trout Lodge," he said flatly. "It sounds good and advertises the fishing." End of discussion. He had business cards printed up with a large, well-hooked Mackinaw leaping in joyous abandon over the ornately scripted Big Trout name, and on the back, a kilted Scot entreating, "Will ye no' come back?" No one could ever figure out the Scotsman, but a lot of the things my father did were incomprehensible to the rest of the world and in the end, it didn't matter anyway. Within a few short seasons the trout fishing, which had been so spectacular at this end of the lake when we arrived, fell off to a degree that made the name a falsehood. And though the immense stock of grayling in the river never seemed to vary over

Gradually and inexorably, the Porsild venture began to take on an air of permanence and respectability.

the years, "Big Grayling Lodge" just didn't seem to inspire much enthusiasm in Dad. Sadly, he allowed the "Big Trout Lodge" cards to run out and by the time they had, he bowed to the inevitable and allowed the common "lodge at Johnson's Crossing" to become the more dignified and specific "Johnson's Crossing Lodge."

And with the name came the tussle to become a bona fide lodge in the literal sense of the word. It was a slow learning process and uphill all the way. Tempers flared, patience was often in short supply and the milk of human kindness flowed thin and blue on occasion. But gradually and inexorably, the old barn began to take on an air of permanence and respectability. And Charlie Taylor's grin deepened, as he brushed the thick hair back from his forehead and marked Bob Porsild's bill with a large, bold PAID, while Arthur P-Jones' superiors said things like, "Good man, that Pettley-Jones!" and looked with satisfaction on the accrued interest from the amortized Johnson's Crossing loan.

A sign erected beside our front entrance advertised home cooking and clean, comfortable rooms. And the trickle was fast becoming a torrent.

14

" I'll take you home again..."

My parents discovered early on that a lodge on the
Alaska Highway could never be the neatly compartmented business that the name implies. Rooms they had, clean and increasingly comfortable with the addition of innerspring mattresses
and running water; a spacious, well-appointed lobby; and opening from it, a dining room serving generous portions of good
food prepared, perhaps not with the elegance of a chef de Cordon
Bleu, but with the instinctive joie de vivre that comes from years
of audacious experimentation. Certainly these three components
justified the "lodge" adjunctive. But even in those early days, it
was obvious that there had to be more. Much more.

In short order, they added a Chevron gas station with a tire
shop as a necessary sideline. The *hygglige* lobby became a meeting hall where politicians could lure prospective voters with the
promise of free coffee and a tasty assortment of Ma Porsild's
Danish pastries. They held dances; requisitioned a movie projec-
tor from the Film Library in Whitehorse to show black and white
National Film Board documentaries, everybody welcome; and,
on occasion, the lobby served as a place of worship when an
itinerant man of the cloth happened by and two or three could be
quickly called together in His name.

A tiny beer parlour built onto the north end of the lodge
came to be a Saturday-night watering hole for our neighbours

from Brook's Brook; Sundays, we were a haven of refuge for hungover participants of the previous evening's intemperance. Hunters and fishermen made the lodge a base of operations, and from time to time we became the temporary headquarters for the RCMP as they mounted a manhunt or search-and-rescue right before our delighted eyes. Mom loaned books and magazines. Dad removed fish hooks from thumbs, thawed frostbitten feet of motorists broken down at forty below and skillfully wrapped accident victims in gauze and bandages, doling out Aspirin and generous belts of overproof rum to the walking wounded. They both offered advice on how to propagate African violets and each was pleased to describe the best way to cook whitefish (Mom suggested filleting, dipping lightly in fine bread crumbs and frying in a luxurious amount of clarified butter; Dad insisted that the *only* way to do it properly was to coat the whole, ungutted fish in thick mud, bury it in hot coals and leave it till the mud dried and cracked off. He cooked it for the family once. It tasted of dirt and dried offal. Dad allowed that a drizzle of seal oil would have made it slide down a tad easier).

As postal service became regular along the highway, first by British Yukon Navigation (BYN) bus line and later by truck transport, the lodge was designated a "mail drop" and edicts regarding schedules, CODs, money orders and the sale of postage stamps came addressed to Dad as "Person in Charge of Mail, 837 Alaska Highway." Mail days were always a highlight, the neighbours gathering around the kitchen table to have coffee while Dad sorted and delivered. Letters were opened on the spot and titillating tidbits of gossip were shared in round-table discussion. Parcels were often divested of their wrappings right then and there and the contents judged by all present. There were few secrets. One enormous box arriving for Joe Henry generated a lot of excitement in the ranks.

A recent cheque for a shipment of fur had been endorsed over to the T. Eaton Company along with an order for a large set of Tesco heavy aluminum pots and pans, a surprise for Kate Henry.

Dad loaded Joe and the carton on the back of the old White and hauled them both across the river. Two days later, Joe came back over for tobacco. Mom greeted him warmly.

"Hello, Joe, how did Kate like her new pots?"

Joe, a wiry little man with a slight speech impediment and a perpetual grin, ducked his head shyly. "She really like them," he stammered. "She cook bi-ig pot moose stew now, you bet." He was quiet for a moment, then blurted, "But gee, Mrs. Bob, them pots sure are *shiny*!"

They laughed together, Joe with delight in their new, mirror-bright cookware, Mom in appreciation of his pleasure. Then she packed up his tobacco, slipped in a couple of bags of hard candy for the kids, and sent him on his way with an admonition to have a care in getting back home.

Mom enjoyed her neighbours, her friends and customers. "Guests," she called them all and was never happier than when she was bustling around finding a gift for that one or doing a favour for the other. Children were always invited into the kitchen and parents lingering over coffee would find them there, up to their elbows in flour and pie dough, or busy shaping buns or washing dishes, one of Mom's big aprons tied under their armpits and knotted twice around. Such helpers were paid off in kisses and a cookie or other treat, but Mom's rewards were the moments shared with her smallest guests, and after their departure she would hasten to deliver their conversational gems.

"Now, what do you think would be straight, and up, with parsley on top?" she would ask, her eyes brimming with mirth.

"Dunno, something to eat? Or what do you mean?" we'd ask.

"That little boy that was just in, I asked him what he wanted and he couldn't think of the name of it but that's how he described it: straight and up with parsley on top." She paused. "Give up?"

"Yep," we'd say. "No idea at all."

"*Cel*-ery!" she'd say. "Straight and up... with parsley on top. It was celery!" And she would return to her kitchen, still chuckling, her round little frame jiggling with enjoyment.

Mom worked a long day, from six in the morning till eleven at night with little time off for good, bad or indifferent behaviour, but she never complained. In fact, she so embraced this way of life that I don't believe she ever felt her life to be lacking in any area. Happiness was the new design of mountains and flowers that Les Allen had drawn around her blackboard menu or a wheelbarrow load of scrap lumber delivered to her old sawhorse behind the beer parlour. Joy was a perfect rendition of the "The Whiffenpoof Song" in three-part harmony during an impromptu concert involving Harry George and some of his cronies up from Brook's for a Sunday visit. Satisfaction was a full house with everyone tucked in and the first faint snores drifting down the hall. And payment was the tall, sour-looking American who turned at the door to tell her, "Those were mighty good groceries, Ma'am." She filled her days with endless chores and her idea of relaxation was to turn that barrow load of scraps into kindling. She wrote long, humorous letters to friends and family and, seemingly, to every third person who stopped over with us. Most evenings, after supper and before the nightly singsong, she would sit at her mangle, a knee-operated electric ironer, smoothing miles of folded linen, holding court with a couple of ladies from Iowa or Arkansas or California whose husbands were down under the bridge fishing for grayling.

As their gas pumps were of 1940 vintage, their power plant ancient, their furniture second-, often third- or fourth-hand, so was Mom's kitchen equipment. She did all her cooking on the old army cookstove with no grill, a wood-devouring, smoke-belching, recalcitrant old son of a bituminous coal burner. Her refrigerator was a scabby Orange Crush pop cooler that alternately flash-froze or parboiled its contents, depending on its whim. And she washed her floor every morning right after the breakfast rush was over, all eighteen hundred square feet of it, with a tiny cellulose string mop. "None of those fancy doodads for me, thank you very much!" she stated when Dad offered to buy her an electric floor washer. Ignoring her remark, he went ahead and bought one anyway. She refused to use it. Dad was incensed. "Alright," he said through tight lips, "I'll do it myself." And off he went to set up the machine, all the while muttering under his breath about stubborn women.

The demonstration was not a roaring success.

When the salesman had shown Dad the advantages of having an automatic floor scrubber, he had used a small area, about two feet square. First, he filled the machine, about the size and shape of an undernourished upright vacuum cleaner, with a quart of hot, soapy water. A pull on the trigger released about a cupful onto the floor. Letting go the trigger, he pressed a switch that activated a pair of revolving brushes. After the brushes loosened the dirt, another trigger was pulled, this one creating a vacuum effect to suck up the dirty water into another container just below the clean-water receptacle. Moving the washer to the side, the salesman had invited Dad to take his white handkerchief to the spot. "You find any dirt where I've scrubbed and I'll *give* you the machine!"

Dad called Mom over. "Look at this," he said, indicating the speckless patch. "You see any dirt?"

Mom had to admit that the spot was lovely but, "Bubi, see how long it takes!"

"Just a matter of getting used to it, you watch."

I'll say this for my father: he was no quitter. He washed that whole floor, lobby, dining room and kitchen, with that little machine. He emptied out the dirty water and filled up with clean about thirty times. He ended up with four electrical extensions before he could reach into every corner. He ran out of the soap powder the salesman had thrown in as a gesture of goodwill; ran off a poor old tourist who had dared to observe that there must be a better way to clean such a big area; and ran up his blood pressure to a degree that Jo privately likened to the point where the Cooker usually blew its cork. It took Dad almost two hours and when he was finished, he carefully cleaned the machine, rinsing out the water containers and wiping down the rest of it. Then he removed the extra extensions, wrapped the cord neatly around the handy-dandy little glitches provided, and thrust the scrubber behind the door in the back porch.

It stayed there for several years, gathering dust in the summer and frost in the winter. Then one year, during spring cleanup, it disappeared. No one ever said where it went, nor did anyone ask. Mom washed her floors with her spaghetti mop and Dad said nothing. He was too busy trying to figure out how to make their new water-driven potato peeler work.

Dad was always a soft touch for the drummers hawking their gizmos and gimcracks, and over the years he amassed a small fortune in labour-saving devices that subtracted nothing from the workload but added much to day-to-day conversation. "Oh no," Mom would groan. "Bob, what are we going to do with a spring-loaded eavestrough cleaner? We don't even have an eavestrough!" And Dad would grin sheepishly and chase her around the kitchen with the gadget while the rest of us would laugh and cheer him on.

Les Allen, who came to work for Dad after he and his partner dissolved their relationship, would examine the latest novelty for possible incorporation into the plumbing or even the decor. "Look at this, Ma," he enthused, indicating the hydraulic potato denuder. "'Twould be summat fine in the flow'r bed. Run a bit of water through it, ye'll 'ave a bleedin' fountain, you would 'n all." Les had spent a couple of years in Burma as an airframe engineer in the RAF, and after the war had immigrated to Canada's North, eventually to Johnson's Crossing. He was one of those rare people who are both practical and artistic, and his presence in the lodge was soon in evidence everywhere.

Les not only decorated Mom's menus, but adorned plant pots, footstools, door frames and garbage cans with colourful flora and fauna. Tasteful watercolours of demure nudes and ruminating bovines hung cheek by jowl in the beer parlour and the hand-lettered sign that directed traffic upstairs, first door to the left, was changed from a bald "Toilet" with an arrow to a more genteel "Washroom" with a pointing hand neatly clad in a white glove featuring a black button on the cuff. Together, he and Dad painted the old barn white with red trim and replaced the black tarpaper with bright blue asphalt shingles. They planted prizewinning gladioli, and together harvested their bumper tomato crops. And when Les stumbled on a mile of abandoned two-inch pipe left over from the gas pipeline that had run from Whitehorse to Watson Lake during the building of the highway, he first claimed it, then sold it to Dad for a bottle of Drambuie to build a water line from the river to the lodge. They were still hauling water from Brook's, summer and winter. With a line to the river, during the summer at least, water could be pumped into a holding tank in the basement. And with more water in the basement, why not pipe it elsewhere, like, say, to the rooms upstairs. Why not, indeed? And maybe heat it too, while we're at it.

Dad and Les were not that experienced in plumbing, but help was close to hand. Betty's Bill was a fireman by vocation but he was also a journeyman plumber, and for the next month his weekends and days off were spent installing pipes and fixtures. Now all that remained was to purchase and set up a water heater. The trusty T. Eaton catalogue was consulted; a twenty-gallon tank was ordered and, in due course, delivered by BYN freight. It was beautiful, gleaming white enamel with a navy-blue crest bearing the words "John Wood Company Limited" in silver script. And it brought its own problem.

"Where will you put it?" Mom asked, innocently enough, as the three of them stood contemplating their new toy.

"Right over here, by the front counter," Dad said. "Right where everyone can see it."

Les laughed dutifully at the joke, then he suggested the upstairs bathroom for its new home.

"No, it's not going upstairs where nobody can see it, it's going right here where I said." Dad pointed with his cigar. Mom and Les looked at each other in dismay. He really meant to put the heater in the middle of the kitchen, in full view of the dining room.

"Ah Bubi, no. We can't have it right there. What would people think to have to look all day at a hot water heater? And see how it would be in the way. *Kom sa*, come on now, let's put it upstairs," Mom coaxed.

The thing was, of course, that excluding the battleship linoleum for which Dad had gone into hock right up to his bushy
blond eyebrows, the Wood electric heater was the first brand new
piece of equipment they had ever purchased. And it was expen-
sive, and functionally pleasing to the eye, and the colour scheme
of white and navy was Dad's favourite and, anyway, it was his
lodge and he could have his heater anywhere he pleased, dammit!

Eventually, with great tact and diplomacy, Mom and Les
were able to persuade Dad to build a nice solid stand for it in the
corner of the bathroom and, in the end, Dad got the maximum
enjoyment out of it after all. He was the one who rented out the
rooms and it was his practice to personally show his guests up to
their accommodation. Everyone was then hauled over to view the
washroom facilities, which included a good-looking John Wood
water heater, "twenty gallons of piping hot water." *Pat, pat* on its
smoothly plump side. "It's brand new, you know." And he'd open
a shiny faucet and let the steaming cascade gush forth for the edi-
fication and entertainment of his admiring and captive audience.
Even when Dad lost, he won.

By the mid-'50s, the work of establishing their "tourist lodge"
was essentially done. Business had settled into a satisfying and
manageable routine. Aksel had graduated from school in Whitehorse and was working for the highways department at Brook's.
Jo and I were boarding out to attend high school, and returning
home weekends and holidays, as Betty had done during our first
years on the highway. There was an order to their days and an
order to their life and after all their years of roaming, there was a
feeling of having found their niche. And it felt good.

Late one clear November afternoon, Mom stood gazing past
the frost-patterned window at the wonderland just beyond the
farthest border of their snow-covered lawn. Across the valley, the
last rays of a dying winter sun turned the Canol mountains into
low rolls of pink cotton against a pearl-grey sky. The nearly full
moon poised briefly on the crest of a rosy hummock before rising
to illuminate the snow-burdened spruce and pine that marched

The view looking over Johnson's Crossing shows the Teslin River Bridge with Mount Oop sparkling in the background.

in precise regiments down the slope to the river. A willow grouse fed on leaf buds on the big poplar at the end of the lawn. Inside, Jiggs-the-cat sat in an empty White Owl box on the desk, chattering out his desire for the fat, clumsy bird.

Dad put down his paper. "What are you looking at, skat?"

Mom turned, smiled. "Oh, I was just seeing how pretty it all is. It reminds me of the Sixtymile." They were both silent, remembering the Bush years. "I wish my mother could have seen this, she would have loved it." Her mother had died while they were living on the Sixtymile; Dad's mother, a few months later. "Bob," she turned to him impulsively. "Let's go home. For a visit."

He said nothing for a long moment. He cleared his throat. "I don't think we can afford it," he said at last.

Mom left the room and returned in an instant, carrying her canvas "sock" into which she squirreled her two-dollar bills and American silver dollars. "Here," she said, dumping it all out on the desk, the heavy coins falling in a shower in front of Jiggs' indignant nose, the pinky-brown bills fluttering more slowly into a drift that threatened to cover the rest of him. "I don't know how much there is but there should be enough."

As Jiggs cursed and haughtily removed himself from the scene lest he be further associated with such a vulgar show of wealth, Dad rose slowly from his chair, his face a study in amazement. "What's this, Elly? Where did all this come from?" he stuttered.

"Oh," Mom said airily, "from here and there, now and then." She laughed. "*Kom sa*, help me count it."

Together, they counted it into stacks of silver, piles of paper. "...two thousand five, two thousand six, two thousand seven dollars!" Dad exclaimed. "I can't believe that you saved all this!"

"And fifty cents," Mom chuckled, holding up the large Canadian coin. "Now... can we go?"

Two months later, a newspaper in Copenhagen carried the following headline:

"Yukon Hotelejer Porsild og Kone Vende Tilbage"

(Yukon Hotel Owner and Wife Come Home)

"*Fra Gronland til Danmark til rensdyr stilling til Yukon guldfelt til turist hus paa Alaska Landevej...* From Greenland to Denmark to reindeer station to Yukon goldfield to tourist lodge on the Alaska Highway, Thorbjorn and his wife, Elly, have done it all. Born in Copenhagen but raised in Greenland, Porsild...."

I STOOD UP, CRAMPED AND CHILLED *from sitting on the cold concrete. The sun had set and the coolness was turning into a chill.* "I'm sorry to have bent your ear for so long. Once I get the bit in my teeth it's kinda hard to get me to whoa!"

Denise smiled. "I enjoyed it," she said. "I almost feel as if I had been there with you."

We turned in at the entrance and paused for a moment to say our goodnights. As I walked on, she called after me, "And what about you? Do you think that you'll ever sell the place and move away?"

I looked back and laughed. "Naw," I said, "I could never leave here, it's all I am and it's all I know." I waved as I started away once more, then looked back at my new friend. "Besides," I called over my shoulder, "if I ever left here, who would look after the cinnamon mine?"

EPILOGUE

AKSEL AND I NEVER BUILT OUR rusty brick house, nor did we raise even one Doberman.

In the fall of 1955, I married Philip Davignon, a tall, slim farmer from Alberta. It was my plan that he should take me away from all this, transplant me into the fertile black earth of Legal, a French farming community near Edmonton, and teach me the fine art of milking cows, collecting eggs and pitching manure. I was going to unlearn pumping gas, slinging hash and marking up souvenirs. Across the lobby of the lodge I walked, enveloped in a vision of a snug farmhouse on the edge of a rolling field of grain. And there I'd be, a blonde and rosy young woman in checked gingham, feeding the chickens that clustered adoringly about my feet, while my smiling, brown-haired husband looked on with loving admiration.

So much for visions.

Instead of the snug farmhouse, there was the drafty, rambling Johnson's Crossing Lodge building. The roses have long since faded and the blonde braids have been whacked off, leaving an unruly mop darkened to a hen-poo brindle. The only crop we raised was an undetermined number of offspring. The tall husband often as not regarded me grumpily as I outlined yet another plan for the business. It wasn't what I wanted. It was what I got.

In the fall of 1955, I married Philip Davignon, a tall, slim farmer from Alberta. It was my plan that he should take me away from all this, but buyers did not leap out of the woodwork.

Mom and Dad ran the lodge for almost eighteen years. In some ways, things got easier: the building part was done, the business well established, their family grown. But though the years on the highway had rewarded them with uncounted hours of enjoyment and a comfortable, if not particularly affluent, lifestyle, it also exacted its toll in health and spirit. In the late '50s, Dad developed asthma and it plagued him the rest of his days, sapping his patience and spirit. Over the next several years Dad's health waned and so did his interest and participation in the business, and the brunt of it fell onto Mom's shoulders. She became uncharacteristically snappy, and worry etched deep lines in her smooth face and put shadows under her eyes. Inevitably, they came to the conclusion: it was time to sell.

Naturally, they hoped that one of their children would show an interest in taking it over, but none seemed of a mind to take

Bob holds his first grandchild, Toby Robert Davignon, in 1957.

it on. We had grown up in the trade, as it were, and were fully aware of the shackles it imposed. Long, grinding hours with little in the bank to ease the ache of overtaxed bones and muscles; short chains tying you to stove and gas pump; no time for yourself; and, always, the endless catering to a demanding travelling public. It's a tough racket at the best of times and we had seen enough to know that there were as many bad times as good.

Phil and I stayed on after we got married. "Just for a year," Phil said, "to give your folks a hand until they find a buyer."

Buyers did not leap from the woodwork and after ten years, Phil sat me down for some serious dialogue. "I think we should buy the lodge ourselves," he said with a straight face.

"Are you out of your mind?" I screeched. "Over my dead body!"

On May 1, 1965, we signed the final papers and took over, lock, stock and barrel. Phil peered into my less-than-joyful face. "Come on, old girl, cheer up. We'll just keep it for five years, get a little ahead, then sell it again."

In fact, we kept it five times that promised "five years" plus a few more before finally listing it for sale when we realized that not one of our own children was going to bite the bullet and save us from ourselves. We did change it, however, after operating it in the traditional style for thirteen years. We closed the dining room and guest rooms, turned the lobby into a store and bake shop, and developed a campground where the neat rows of prefabs had once lined up for inspection. It was an easier, less-hectic business—long hours still, but we closed up shop in the winter and that made a world of difference.

⋅ఌ⃛ ⊰

After their retirement, Mom and Dad moved back to Whitehorse. There was no problem trying to find something to do with their hands. For many years, Erling had been director of the herbarium

After thirteen years, we did make some changes, turning the lobby into a store and bake shop.

Loaves of bread were baked fresh each day and brought golden brown and steaming from the kitchen.

in the National Museum in Ottawa. Once again he called on his big brother. "We need some specimens from the Dempster area. Do you remember how to collect them?" The Dempster was a section of north-central Yukon about which little was known. Dad was delighted to accept the contract. "It's the chance of a lifetime in an interesting area," he told us. "The Ogilvies were never glaciated and plants grow there that won't grow in the silt banks of lower altitudes. And the climate is different. Of course we'll go."

And go they did. For three summers in a row, they loaded up their camper and headed up the Dempster Highway. Their expeditions were successful beyond all expectations for they found fifty species formerly unreported in the Yukon, gathering miles past the end of the road, which was still under construction, and into the mountains up to the 6,500-foot level. During those summers they collected 464 different species, four to twenty specimens of each, the extra sets to be used for exchange with museums and universities in Scandinavia, the Soviet Union and Alaska. When they could collect ripe seed from rare plants, these were sprouted under controlled conditions in Ottawa. Many of them were grasses, Dad's special interest that dated back to those bucolic days with Erling on the reindeer project.

The summers on the Dempster were like a paid holiday for the folks: camping out, climbing mountains, paddling out after an elusive water lily in a still, green pond. Rest, fresh air and the change of pace helped to revitalize them both. But the contract was for three years only and when it ended, Mom and Dad settled into community life in Whitehorse with the same vigour and zest that had underscored all their previous adventures.

Dad died in his sleep just a few days after his seventy-ninth birthday, quietly and without fuss. He had been in declining health for a couple of years, was weary of our fast-changing world and badly hurt by the news of Erling's death a few months previously. His passing was a release, a natural progression from a life that had become a burden to a reward that would surely include broad mountain meadows bright with his beloved Arctic flowers, and abundant grasses to study and catalogue.

Shortly after Dad's death, Mom sold their house and moved into an apartment, alone but as busy and fiercely independent as she ever was. In time, arthritis and cataracts slowed her pace but not enough to diminish her enthusiasm for the new and unknown and she never hesitated to commit herself to anything, from a position on the advisory board for the Council on Aging to a community Participaction contest with Yellowknife, capital of the Northwest Territories. Nor did she miss an opportunity to come out and lend a hand on the counter, selling my home baking.

Alternately cajoling and bullying my intimidated customers, she would sell everything and then hustle out to the kitchen with the empty trays. "Fill 'em up!" she would command, winking at Phil with both eyes while I groaned and started over.

"Jeez, Mom," I would whine. "Gimme a break, I've been at this all morning."

"Too bad. You told me to get out there and sell and I have. Sorry 'bout that. Here, what's the matter with these?" she once asked, picking up a tray full of meat pies that had been forgotten in a too-hot oven. "*Skit med dedt*, to heck with that, I'll sell them anyway."

"No, Ma..." But it was too late and she went out there flogging the burnt pies as if there were no tomorrow. And probably marking them up two bits more than I usually asked. "You don't charge enough. How can you make enough money to keep me in my old age like that?" she would tease.

One September, Dad's youngest brother Sten and his wife, Lene, came to visit for the first time. He was so like Dad in many ways, tall and ruddy, with traces of ginger in his thinning hair. We walked across the bridge, chatting about Dad, his life and his accomplishments. As we turned to retrace our steps, the sun broke from its cloud cover and shone brightly, illuminating the valley. High up on the west bank of the river, nestled in its setting of poplar touched golden by an early frost, was the lodge, as solid and square as the man who had built it. It was still not a lovely building, but there was a weathered permanence to it. Sten stood still, gazing at the building.

"What are you thinking?" I asked him.

He smiled. "On one of your father's trips home to Denmark, I asked him if he ever thought of coming back to stay. 'Oh no,' he replied. 'I could never come back here. I am a part of the Yukon.' Now I know what he meant."

❧❀☙

Nearly twenty years later, Sten's line returns to tickle my memory as I kick back the old rump-sprung recliner and relax in the living room of my comfortable little home. It is set high on the hill above Whitehorse proper and from the kitchen window I can look out over the Yukon River Valley where we and the Pinchin brothers had played out our youthful games and adventures. I can't see the river, but its blue-green moiré surface swirls through my mind at will, providing a background for a retrospection of the years that have passed.

Phil and I sold the Lodge—Johnson's Crossing Campground Service by then—in May 1992. Ironically, in a converse re-enactment of that earlier confrontation when Phil had sought to convince me of the advisability of buying the lodge, this time I didn't screech, but through all of his blandishments I stood there shaking my head and scuffling my feet, steadfastly refusing to even consider selling it.

After being dragged, kicking and screeching, into ownership of Johnson's Crossing Lodge, it had taken me a few years to come to an appreciation of the business that was more lifestyle than life work. But finally, I had embraced it and like my mother, had put my own stamp on the quality of its production and felt I had more to give. "I've still got some good years left," I told him.

And I had. But Phil didn't.

Phil was a child of the Depression. His mother had died when he was only six and he and his three brothers had been raised in a succession of foster homes and turfed out early to care for themselves. He had worked for a living from the time he was old enough to lift a forkful of manure or hold the reins of a team of horses. He had been a farmhand, miner, truck driver, mechanic, and finally, the jack-of-every-trade-in-the-book that the owner-operator of a highway business must be. And after nearly sixty years of it, he was just plain tired.

I managed to hold out for another couple of seasons, but finally capitulated and we listed the old place for sale in the spring of 1991. That fall, a construction company from Fort Nelson arrived to make repairs to the decking of the Teslin River Bridge. "We're looking to buy a summer business on the highway," were the first words contractor Gordon Smith said to me. "I understand yours is for sale?"

Phil was a child of the Depression: he had worked as a jack-of-all-trades since he was old enough to lift a pitchfork, and now he was just plain tired.

And it was that easy.

Within a few months of the sale, Phil and I were ensconced on a very nice lot in Arkell, a brand new subdivision of Whitehorse that developed around us even as we put down tender new roots and attempted to infuse the cosy ambiance of the Old Barn into a large mobile home with a good-sized addition. We missed Johnson's Crossing and our previous lifestyle, but it helped that all of our children, most now with partners and children, had all settled in Whitehorse. That gave Aksel, whose own family had scattered far and wide, a good laugh.

"Can you believe that?" he chortled. "Lived all their young lives in Johnson's Crossing and given the chance to go, end up eighty miles from where they grew up! And, on a clear and calm day, within halloo-ing distance of you and Phil." The fact is, every one of them is a Yukoner born and bred, each settled into the community with no desire to live elsewhere.

Phil had looked forward to our retirement and threw himself wholeheartedly into serious unemployment.

Life after the lodge was pretty good, for the most part. I could never talk Phil into travelling, but I managed to do a little bit on my own: Nova Scotia and Prince Edward Island on the east coast of Canada and most of Vancouver Island and Haida Gwaii on the west; New Zealand; Arizona; and New Mexico. And in 2006, Aksel and I and some of our children, along with several Danish cousins, went to Disko Island on the west side of Greenland for an anniversary celebration of the arctic research station that Morton P. had started a hundred years earlier. As we explored the station and the grounds, I took a peek around the back of the station, half expecting to find the chopping block and the axe that Dad had employed in his misadventure with Erling's thumb. It wasn't there.

Unfortunately, those pesky "good years" that I believed I had left came back time after time to haunt me and although I gave a life of leisure a good shot, I was soon casting about for something besides light housekeeping for two to keep me occupied. One day, a "Sales Clerk Wanted" sign in the front window of Mac's

Life after the lodge was good, and I even managed to do some travelling.

Fireweed Books caught my eye. Armed with my years of public relations and dressed in my most clerkish clothes, I applied.

"I've always wanted to work in a bookstore," I told Elaine Smart, the elegant owner of the only bookstore in town.

Well, that was a blatant lie. I'd never given a thought to working in a bookstore or any store other than the one we'd had at JC, for that matter. All I really wanted was something to do that was just a bit more interesting than dusting.

Elaine made it simple. "It will just be part-time help," she told me. "Four hours a day, four days a week to start. If all goes well and more hours open up, we might consider offering them to you."

And with those words, my days of indolence were over and I was to discover that, in fact, I had fourteen more "good years" left. And that blatant lie? Turned out it wasn't a lie after all; I'd just never really put voice to that particular desire.

⛬

Inevitably, there have been other changes in our lives.

Betty and Bill's marriage did not survive a myriad of changes and separations, and Betty remarried in 1958. The six years' age difference that was such a barrier when we were growing up evaporated when we both reached the 29-and-holding pattern, and over the years our relationship deepened into friendship via the reams of wise and witty bulltweet we sent back and forth in care of Canada Post when she left the Yukon. She eventually put down roots in Camrose, Alberta, alone again but within shouting distance of her oldest daughter Elaine and her four grandchildren. Jean, her younger daughter, became a member of the RCMP.

Jo, true to the nature of her spirit, left home early and joined the Canadian Air Force, loving every minute of it and resenting bitterly being turned down for re-enlistment when Canada's forces were rearranged. She married twice, the last time to John Robert Brown, a Seminole from Oklahoma. After shuttling back and forth between Tulsa and Whitehorse, they finally settled in the Yukon with Ayla, their purebred Australian sheepdog; Fritz, a mongrel of dubious parentage; and two cats, Chloe and Smokey.

Aksel, first-class navigator, fishing guide, co-developer of the only cinnamon mine in the world, chum of a thousand plans and schemes, stayed with the Northwest Highway System for thirteen years, eventually fetching up as camp foreman at Swift River. In the late '50s, he married Joyce Bevington. They produced a covey of towheaded youngsters and in 1966 moved to Alberta, where Ax tried his hand in a totally new role, that of gentleman farmer. Except for herds of range cows that we had saved from rustlers, time after time, the closest Ax had ever been to a cow was the picture on the ever-present tin of Pacific milk on our kitchen table, and in the end, the cows defeated him. Gentleman, yes. Farmer, no. So he did the next best thing he could think of: he learned to fly helicopters, eventually becoming a senior pilot with Associated Helicopters in Edmonton.

He and Joyce were divorced in 1985 and he moved to Vancouver Island, where he and a friend bought a small service station.

Aksel married Joyce Bevington and they produced a covey of towheaded youngsters.

"Golly," I would say, "if you're so gung-ho to get back into the service industry after all these years, have I got a place for you!" But he remembered all too well what it was to own a business on the only road through town: on call night and day.

Phil lost a short and intense battle with cancer in 2002 and, a little later, Jo journeyed on without us.

Shortly after we had moved to Whitehorse, Mom fell in her apartment and broke her hip. She was never very mobile after that, and a second fall a few years later and another fractured hip left her confined to a wheelchair. Undaunted, sharp of mind and tongue, she continued to rule her world with the imperious aplomb of any ruler on her throne and even a move to a nursing home failed to dampen that wonderful spirit.

In July of 2004, Mom broke her femur and while she was in the hospital we received the news that Betty had died of complications from diabetes. Mom accepted the news with her usual stoicism, but upon her return to Macaulay Lodge, it became apparent that this last accident had stolen her last vestige of independence, a state of affairs that was not to be borne. Six weeks later, at the age of 101, Mom died in her sleep.

Calm, thoughtful and forthright, she was the touchstone in our lives, showing us by word and example how to get the most out of life. We are fortunate, indeed, to have had such a mother.

The Old Barn went into a genteel decline after we left. An old building constructed in most part of salvaged lumber and with its best years well behind, it did not take kindly to being left unattended and unheated in the winters. After some unsatisfactory dickering with the Yukon Government to restore it as a historic site, Gordon and his partners made the difficult decision to tear it down and rebuild on the same site. And in 1996, they did just that, replacing it with an attractive single-storey structure with much the same layout as the first floor of Dad's "tourist lodge."

Recently, the business changed hands once again and soon after, I went back for a visit with Aksel, who was here on his annual migration north to maintain his Yukoner status. We drove down the side road to the river, parked on the bank above the back eddy where the biggest ling cod and grayling used to lurk, and got out to embark on a sentimental walkabout.

The first port of call was to the site where our old friend, the barge, had lain in dry dock for more than twenty years. It was no longer there, of course. In the mid-'60s, the barge—raft, ferry, battleship, conveyance of choice that it had been to us—had finally given in to the blandishments of the mighty Teslin River in full spring runoff and had floated, high, wide, and handsome, downstream on one last adventure. We mused for a time on its probable final moments and destination before walking on. From the riverbank, we wandered over to Jackson's fish camp, still in use from time to time from the looks of the woodpile and tent frames, and down to the little creek where we had learned to swim. Willow and scrub brush had overgrown the banks of the little watercourse, but the creek, clear and cool, was as inviting as it had been when we'd stripped to our underwear and shocked Mrs. Wing into fits and starts.

Later, we walked across the bridge to check out the cinnamon mine. It is still just a blot of rusty sand in the middle of the cutbank, but it remains charged with possibility, awaiting only the arrival of a new crop of young explorers. And as we stood there remembering, I heard again my sister's soft purr, as she geared her little piece of wood down into low and began clearing away rubble.

Eventually, we drove up to the—what? I asked Ax. "Not the lodge. Certainly not the Old Barn. I wonder how they describe the new place?" We didn't know, and when we got there I didn't think to ask. But I was pleasantly surprised by the feeling of homecoming. Perhaps it was the configuration of the interior of the new building, so like our old place. Maybe it was the homey smell of bread baking, the tourists nattering over their coffee and cinnamon buns, or the glimpse of industrious to-ing and fro-ing in the open concept kitchen. Whatever it was, it was a little bit like stepping into the past. I almost expected to hear young voices raised in harmony over the rattling of dishes being washed.

After coffee and a chat with the new owners, we started for home. As we drove out of the valley, I turned and looked back the way we'd come.

From the top of the hill I could see what we had seen all those years ago at the very start of our JC adventure: the long bridge spanning the broad blue river and the clay banks rising high and glowing golden in the slanting rays of the late afternoon sun. The clearing that had once been filled with row upon row of potential bowling alleys now showed camping spots. And on the river side of the clearing is that good-looking new... inn, maybe. Turning to face the front, I thought again of the old lodge, remembering that un-pretty old building that had provided both shelter and industry for forty-five years, and the two good people who had turned the industry into a lifestyle, the shelter into a home. Above all else I remember the love and laughter that permeated that home and the music that filled it every evening. And in remembering, I am filled and sustained by the essence of those happy seasons of the heart.

Whatever made me think that I could have been contented with all those cows and chickens?

ABOUT THE AUTHOR

ELLEN MARGRETHE DAVIGNON née Porsild was born at St. Mary's Hospital in Dawson on October 22, 1937, when her parents mined and trapped in the Sixtymile area.

She moved, with her family, to Whitehorse in 1943 and subsequently to Johnson's Crossing five years later. Here, from an abandoned US Army camp, her father built the Johnson's Crossing Lodge, a lifestyle enterprise that remained in the family for forty-five years.

She married Philip Davignon (from Legal, Alberta) in her parents' lodge in October 1955. Ten years later, she and Phil bought the Old Barn (as the family affectionately refers to it). They continued to run the operation, altering services from time to time to suit the changing needs of the highway. Their five children were "raised in the business," and became a part of it from the time they were able to hold the door open and greet prospective customers. All have fond memories of their "Lodge" upbringing and credit it with teaching them good work ethics as well as a certain easy way with a conversation or anecdote.

For their last fourteen years in public service, Ellen and Phil ran their business as Johnson's Crossing Campground Services. Instead of rooms, they rented out camp spots, and in place of a restaurant, Ellen worked her adult version of a cinnamon mine. With over seven tons of flour, and not just a little cinnamon, each summer her oven produced thousands of buns, cinnamon and otherwise, bread pies and other baked goods for the travelling public. "It was a happy kind of business; everyone left with a smile on his face," Ellen remembers fondly.

Today, she produces an occasional batch of cinnamon buns or meat pies for family gatherings or the odd bake sale, just enough to keep her hand in, she says. "With a whole raft of grandkids nearly grown and looking for adventure, you never know when the urge to get into the old family business might strike. I want to be ready."

The cinnamon mine is just rusty sand in the cutbank, but it awaits only a new crop of young explorers.

Northern titles from Harbour Publishing
www.harbourpublishing.com

I MARRIED THE KLONDIKE
by Laura Beatrice Berton
ISBN: 978-1-55017-333-8
Paperback / 5.25 x 8 / 232 pp / 2005

In 1907, Laura Beatrice Berton, a 29-year-old kindergarten teacher, left her comfortable life in Toronto, Ontario, to teach in a Yukon mining town. She fell in love with the North—and with a northerner—and made Dawson City her home for the next 25 years. Her classic and enduring memoir tells of memorable characters in a town that was nicknamed the "Paris of the North" because although the gold rush was over, the townsfolk still clung to the lavishness of the city's golden era. The young teacher soon found herself hosting tea parties, attending formal dinners, dancing the minuet at fancy balls and going on elaborate sleighing parties. In the background, a famous poet wrote ballads on his cabin wall, an archbishop lost on the tundra ate his boots to survive and men living on dreams of riches grew old panning the creeks for gold. Humourous, poignant and filled with stories of both drudgery and decadence, this is an unforgettable book by a brave and intelligent woman.

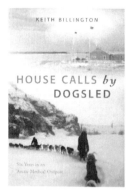

HOUSE CALLS BY DOGSLED
Six Years in an Arctic Medical Outpost
by Keith Billington
ISBN: 978-1-55017-423-6
Paperback / 6 x 9 / 344 pp / 2008

Keith Billington, a nurse, and his wife Muriel, a midwife, arrived in the Northwest Territories outpost of Fort McPherson, in mid-September 1964. Barely into their twenties, these two young professionals were all the medical help available to the Gwich'in people, who taught them how to snowshoe, choose a dog team and live off the land. They experienced the births of babies and the tragic deaths of other children, were the first to tend gun-shot victims and deal with illnesses made worse by the isolation. Their story also tells of caribou hunts, fishing in summer lakes and travelling in winter by dog team, of sun-returning parties, and of drum-dancing and New Year feasts. This is a delightfully warm celebration of the North in the days just before skidoos and cell phones took the edge off the isolation.

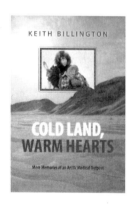

COLD LAND, WARM HEARTS
More Memories of
an Arctic Medical Outpost
by Keith Billington
ISBN: 978-1-55017-534-9
Hardback / 6 x 9 / 296 pp / 2010

Billington dishes up more of the hair-raising and heartwarming stories about medical emergencies and Native traditions that made his first book such a hit. In this book Keith and Muriel return to their northern haunts after the passage of more than a quarter century and learn the endings to many of the stories started in the first book. They are moved beyond tears to discover their old medical post in Fort McPherson replaced by a modern two-storey facility named for their faithful Gwich'in assistant, William Firth. Grippingly written and infused with great warmth, this is an absorbing adventure story that rounds out the Billingtons' Arctic saga with a deepened understanding of the far North and its people.

HISTORY HUNTING IN THE YUKON
by Michael Gates
ISBN: 978-1-55017-477-9
Paperback / 6 x 9 / 256 pp / 2010

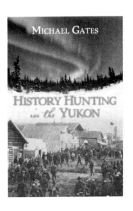

Conspiracies to overthrow the Yukon; terrorism in the Klondike; a bigamist Klondike Casanova; gunfights and how the Mounties got their man; Robert Service's secret love life; the Canadian who fooled Alaskans into making him governor; floods, famine and things found frozen from the past—the Yukon has them all—and more! Dipping into his personal experiences and a 40-year love affair with Yukon history, author Michael Gates takes us on a journey to some of the places, people and events that make the Yukon eternally captivating. Discover the colourful stories and deeper legacy of human history that has occurred upon this remote and expansive territory.

HILLS OF SILVER
The Yukon's Mighty Keno Hill Mine
by Dr. Aaro E. Aho
ISBN: 978-1-55017-394-9
Paperback / 6 x 9 / 320 pp / 2006

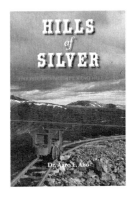

The fabulously rich Keno Hill silver deposit, discovered in 1918, made the Yukon one of the world's leading silver producers and backstopped the territorial economy for decades. As the Klondike strike gave rise to the boom town of Dawson, the Keno strike fostered feisty Keno City, the last of the wild west mining towns: "Down in shacks by Lightning Creek, vintners and vendors of moonshine and the sporting girls catered to the miners on weekends amid scratching gramophone melodies." The story of Keno's discovery, development and decline is one of the great adventures of the North, and it is told here by one of the Yukon's legendary mining personalities, Dr. Aaro Aho, whose authoritative voice on mining matters is nicely offset by his taste for juicy gossip.

REMARKABLE YUKON WOMEN
profiles by Claire Festel, portraits by Valerie Hodgson
ISBN 13: 978-1-55017-523-3
Paperback / 8 x 10 / 112 pp / 2011

The Yukon is a mythic place—the land is vast and wild, the climate harsh and uncompromising, the people resourceful and resilient. The stories in this book, shared by fifty women—"born here or came here"—attest to the enduring nature of the North and the evolving character of a dynamic community. The changes over time and the things that stay the same give a unique insight into the circumstances that make their lives different. Each of these stories, beautifully illustrated with a full-colour portrait of the woman profiled, paints a picture of what life was—and is—really like for Yukon women. It is an untold story that will deepen your understanding of how and why this remote frontier adds not just colour, but depth, sensitivity and strength to the Canadian story.